MEL BAY PRESENTS

JAZZ THEORY HANDBOOK

MW01091942

BY PETER SPITZER

CD CONTENTS

MEL BAY ®

Visit us on the Web at www.melbay.com — E-mail us at email@melbay.com

1 2 3 4 5 6 7 8 9 0

Table of Contents

Introduction

Jazz Theory Handbook is the product of 30 years of teaching, performing, and study. I have tried to provide a source of information that is clear and concise, and at the same time complete, presented in a way that puts theory into a practical, realistic perspective.

This book will help you to understand how contemporary jazz players think, and to apply theory concepts in your own playing. After you have finished this book, you should also be well prepared to understand any other jazz theory method.

We will introduce subjects progressively, with each new one based on those introduced before. Review ideas that are already familiar, until you reach the "new information" level appropriate for yourself. At the end of each chapter are playing and writing exercises that will help you to internalize and apply theory concepts.

The CD that accompanies this book includes all the musical examples, and three play-along tracks. Be sure to listen to all the examples. Better yet, play (or sing) the examples yourself as well, preferably on piano. No matter what your instrument, you should develop some keyboard skills.

The best way to fluency is through actual playing experience. To benefit most from this book you should also have a good fake book, and other musicians with whom to practice. Play-along recordings or software can be useful if you don't have this opportunity.

Of course, musical creativity comes from a deeper source than just theory. But music theory is a powerful tool. It will sharpen your thinking and hearing, and will maximize your creative potential.

Musicians on the CD
Murray Low — piano
John Shifflett — bass
Wally Schnalle — drums
Peter Spitzer — tenor sax

Recorded at OTR Studios, Belmont, California
Cookie Marenco — Engineer

Special thanks to Ragnar Gilberts, Jackie McLean, Bob Murphy, Patricia Musgrave, Larry Sweet, Jim Witzel, and the many students and colleagues who played a part in developing this book; and my deep appreciation to the teachers who shaped my outlook: David Baker, Eddy Flenner, and Joe Henderson.

Chapter 1

Intervals and Scales

In this chapter, we will review the fundamental elements of music: intervals, major scales, and minor scales. Even if you are already familiar with these ideas, read this chapter carefully; it will serve as a basis for everything that follows.

All of these concepts are equally valid for jazz, classical, and popular styles.

Play or sing every musical example yourself, listening carefully. You can also hear each example on the CD that accompanies this book.

1. Half steps and whole steps *(example: CD track 1)*

An *interval* is a measurement of the distance between two notes.

A *half step* is the smallest interval in the traditional Western music system.

A *whole step* is two half steps.

2. Major scales *(examples: CD track 1)*

A *scale* is a series of notes, ascending or descending in a certain interval pattern. The most basic, familiar scale is the *major scale.*

Major scales are formed by arranging seven notes within an octave, with half steps between 3-4 and 7-8, the other notes a whole step apart.

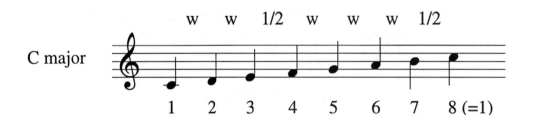

When a piece is said to be "in the key of C major," that means that it uses mostly notes from that scale, with C as the home note (tonic).

In a C major scale (no sharps or flats), the half steps are already between 3-4 (E to F) and 7-8 (B to C). But if we wish to construct major scales from other notes, keeping half steps 3-4 and 7-8, some notes will need to be sharped or flatted. We can do this with a *key signature.* For example:

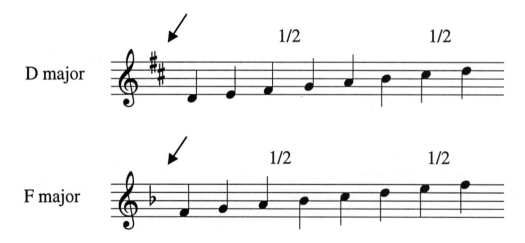

There are exactly 12 different major scales.

The following terms are often used to name the steps ("degrees") of a major scale: *tonic* (1), *supertonic* (2), *median* (3), *subdominant* (4), *dominant* (5), *submediant* (6), and *leading tone* (7).

3. Circle of fifths

This diagram is a convenient way to organize all 12 major scales (or keys) according to how many sharps or flats each contains. It is also called the *cycle of keys, circle of keys, cycle of fifths,* or *circle of fourths.*

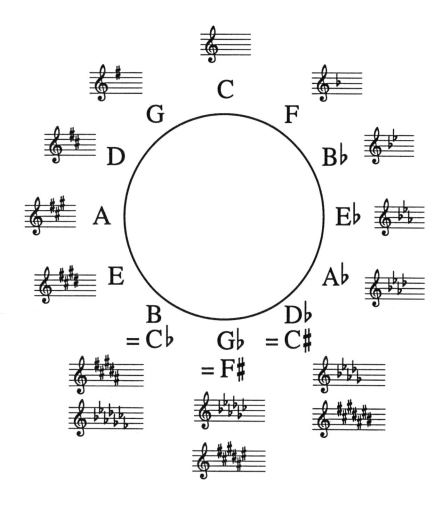

The flats or sharps are always added to a key signature in a certain order. For flats: B♭, E♭, A♭, D♭, G♭, C♭, F♭. For sharps: F♯, C♯, G♯, D♯, A♯, E♯, B♯. Note that the order of sharps is the reverse of the order of flats.

The overlap at the bottom of the circle ("5 o'clock" to "7 o'clock") shows that a scale could go by more than one name.

Memorize the circle, starting from C, moving clockwise. It has other uses, essential in jazz, that we will discuss later.

4. Intervals—how they are named *(examples: CD track 1)*

Interval names have two parts, *quality* and *number* (for example, "minor third"). To find the number: Using the bottom note of the interval as the root ("1") of an imaginary major scale, count the lines and spaces upwards to find whether the interval is a "3rd," "5th," etc.

The quality of an interval is usually *major*, *minor*, *perfect*, *augmented*, or *diminished* (abbreviations: M, m, p, +, d).

If the top note falls naturally within the major scale of the bottom note, then the interval is: *perfect* if a unison, 4th, 5th, or octave; *major* if a 2nd, 3rd, 6th, or 7th.

If the top note is altered (with a sharp, flat or natural) from the note normally found in the scale, then the interval is named as follows:

- a perfect interval raised a half step is *augmented*

- a perfect interval lowered a half step is *diminished*

- a major interval lowered a half step is *minor*

- a major interval raised a half step is *augmented*

- a minor interval lowered a half step is *diminished*

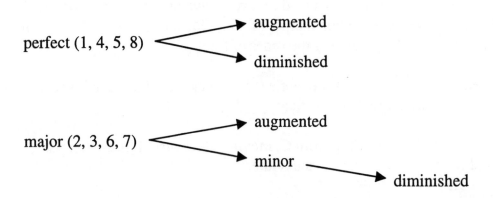

Compare the following intervals to the "scale tone" intervals in the previous example:

Intervals may also be *doubly augmented* or *doubly diminished*:

Intervals larger than an octave (*compound intervals*) are named like their counterparts within an octave.

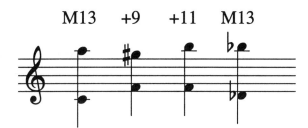

Alternate terminology: Musicians often say "flat" and "sharp" to describe scale tones relative to their natural positions in a major scale. For example, an F♯ above a C might be called a "sharp 4" (♯4), equivalent to the more proper "augmented fourth" (+4).

Intervals that are spelled differently, but sound the same, are called *enharmonic*. For example, +4 and d5 are enharmonic (C to F♯ = C to G♭).

5. Hearing intervals *(examples: CD track 2)*

The opening notes to familiar songs can help you learn to recognize the characteristic sound of each interval:

m2   "Ode to Joy," "Silver Bells," "I'm Getting Sentimental Over You," "Habanera" from the opera *Carmen* (descending)

M2   major scale, "Do Re Mi" (from *The Sound of Music*)

m3   minor triad, Brahms' lullaby, "Greensleeves," "Georgia On My Mind," "Star Spangled Banner" (descending)

M3   major triad, "When the Saints Go Marching In"

p4   "Here Comes the Bride" (wedding march from *Lohengrin*), "Eine Kleine Nachtmusik" (descending)

d5   "Maria," "Cool" (from *West Side Story*), theme from "The Simpsons" TV show (first note to third note)

p5   "Star Wars" theme, "Twinkle Twinkle Little Star"

m6   "Black Orpheus," theme from *Love Story* (descending), "No More Blues" ("Chega de Saudade") (descending)

M6   "My Bonnie," "Take the 'A' Train," "Nobody Knows the Trouble I've Seen" (descending)

m7   "Somewhere" (*West Side Story*), theme to original "Star Trek" TV show, "Watermelon Man" (descending)

M7   "Ceora," "Over the Rainbow" (first note to third note), "Samba d' Orfeo" (first note to fourth note), "I Can't Get Started" (first note to fourth note), "I Love You" (descending)

p8   "Over the Rainbow," "Take Me Out to the Ball Game," "The Christmas Song," "Willow Weep for Me" (descending)

Sometimes it is useful to think of an interval as a combination of smaller intervals. For example:

M2	=	2 half steps
m3	=	1 whole step + 1 half step
M3	=	2 whole steps
p4	=	2 whole steps + 1 half step
d5	=	m3 + m3
p5	=	M3 + m3
m6	=	p5 + 1 half step, or M3 + M3
M6	=	p5 + 1 whole step
m7	=	p5 + m3
M7	=	p5 + M3
p8	=	p5 + p4

6. Minor scales *(examples: CD track 3)*

After major, the next most basic scale in Western music is *minor*. There are five terms associated with minor—*relative*, *parallel*, *natural*, *harmonic*, and *melodic*.

If we pick any major scale, begin on the sixth scale step, then build a one-octave scale using the same notes, we have built the *relative minor* of that major scale.

Each of the 12 major scales thus is paired with a minor scale that shares its key signature (A minor is the *relative minor* of C major; C major is the *relative major* of A minor).

Parallel minor means same root, different scale pattern (C minor is the *parallel minor* of C major).

Finding the relative minor results in a *natural minor* scale—that is, a scale with the interval pattern shown below:

A natural minor

Often, the 7th step of a minor scale will be raised a half step, to provide a leading tone; this results in a *harmonic minor* scale:

A harmonic minor

Melodic minor is shown below. Note that the leading tone (G♯) is present going up, but the sixth (F♯) is raised also, to eliminate the "exotic" augmented second between F and G♯. Going down, melodic is the same as natural minor.

A melodic minor

All of the words that we have defined in this section are used in both classical music and jazz, with one important exception: In jazz, we use the term "melodic minor" to mean only the ascending part of this scale (the first half of the scale shown above).

(A note to those of you who already know chord theory: *Harmonic* minor gets its name from the fact that the raised seventh is introduced for a *harmonic* purpose—to make the V chord dominant, for the required push towards I. *Melodic* minor is named for its use by composers in *melodic* situations, to smooth out the scale while keeping the raised seventh.)

Relative and *parallel* describe the relationship between two scales, not scale structures.

Natural, harmonic, and *melodic* describe scale structures, but it is most accurate to think of these as forms that may be taken by a single (variable) scale. Music written in a minor key will frequently shift from one form to another within the same piece.

Here are the three traditional forms of minor, built from the note C:

Note that these three scales are identical for the first five scale steps; differences occur only on steps 6 and 7.

7. Other scales you should know *(examples: CD track 4)*

Play through the following scales, and listen carefully to their sound. Later in this book we will consider these and other scales in more detail.

8. Transposing *(examples: CD track 4)*

Transposing means moving a piece of music into another key. The structure of the melody and harmony do not change, but the entire piece is moved higher or lower by some interval. The example below shows two measures of melody, first in F major, then transposed to A major (up a M3).

Some instruments are *transposing instruments*. This means that music written for them must be transposed in order to be compatible with the rest of the band or orchestra. Someone playing a B♭ clarinet, for example, cannot read the same music as the piano or flute, but must have his or her part transposed up a M2.

The B♭ clarinet is named that way because its note C sounds like a B♭ on piano. Trumpet, tenor saxophone, soprano saxophone and clarinet are *B♭ instruments*. Alto sax and baritone sax are *E♭ instruments*, meaning that their C sounds like an E♭ on piano. (These are the most common sizes of sax, clarinet, and trumpet. Others exist, including clarinets in A, C, and E♭, saxophones in C, and trumpets in C.)

Instruments that do not transpose are called *C instruments*, or said to be in *concert key*. These include piano, guitar, flute, violin, trombone, and oboe.

To transpose a concert part into one for B♭ clarinet, trumpet, or soprano sax, move it up a whole step. Thus, a piano part in F major would be moved into the key of G major, with each note moved a step higher. Transposing for B♭ tenor sax works the same way, but the tenor part must be written another octave up as well, if you want it to come out in the correct range. To transpose a concert part into one for E♭ alto sax, move both the notes and the key up a major sixth (concert F becomes the alto's D). Baritone sax, another E♭ instrument, works the same way, but must be written another octave up as well, if you want it to sound in the same range.

9. Exercises

- Write the following intervals, above each given note:

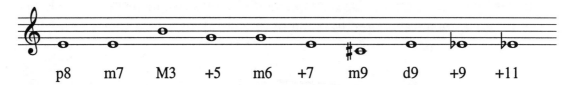

| p8 | m7 | M3 | +5 | m6 | +7 | m9 | d9 | +9 | +11 |

- Identify the intervals between adjacent notes in the following line. Then transpose the same line, beginning on E (use separate manuscript paper). You may either use a new key signature, or write in all accidentals (sharps, flats, or naturals).

- Write out all 12 melodic minor scales, both ascending and descending forms.

- Work on learning to recognize by ear all the intervals and scales covered in this chapter. If possible, find a partner and quiz each other—one plays the interval or scale, the other identifies it.

- Play all 12 major scales, one octave each, up and down. Move roots clockwise along the circle of fifths. If necessary, write the scales first. When you think you are ready, throw the paper away, and play the scales again, from memory. Increase the tempo until you are playing automatically, rather than thinking of each note.

- Practice making up melodies in each major and minor key. The ideas do not have to be memorable; the object is to loosen up your creative process. Do this on your instrument, not on paper.

- Make up a short phrase ("lick") based on a major or minor scale, and learn it in all 12 keys. Think numbers. For example:

Chapter 2

Chord Building

Using the concepts presented in Chapter 1, we can now learn how chords are constructed.

This chapter is a rather condensed presentation of chord building—you should memorize every concept.

Be sure to listen to every example on the CD, and if possible, play or sing every example yourself.

1. Triads *(examples: CD track 5)*

A *chord* is a group of notes sounded simultaneously, usually arranged in intervals of consecutive thirds, above a *root*. A three-note chord is called a *triad*. There are four types of triads: *major, minor, augmented,* and *diminished*. The table below shows how each type of triad is constructed:

major (C)	minor (Cm)	augmented (C+)	diminished (Cdim)
p5	p5	+5	d5
M3	m3	M3	m3
root	root	root	root

2. Seventh chord vocabulary *(examples: CD track 5)*

A four-note chord, arranged in thirds, is called a *seventh chord*. In jazz, seventh chords are the basic chordal unit (although ninth, eleventh, and thirteenth chords are also used, as well as triads). This contrasts with classical usage, where triads are usually the basic unit. The following table shows how to build the most common types of seventh chords.

major seven (Cmaj7)	dominant seven (C7)	minor seven (Cm7)	minor seven flat five (Cm7♭5)	diminished seven (Cdim7)	augmented seven (C7+)	sus 4 (C7sus4)
M7	m7	m7	m7	d7	m7	m7
p5	p5	p5	d5	d5	+5	p5
M3	M3	m3	m3	m3	M3	p4
root	root	root	root	root	root	root

Here are some additional chord types that you should know:

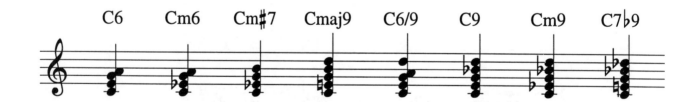

Chord symbol notation is not completely standardized; below are some alternate notations that you may encounter:

Cmaj7 = CM7 = CΔ7 = CΔ

Cm7 = Cmi7 = C–7

Cm7$\flat$5 = C$^{\emptyset}$ ("half diminished")

Cdim7 = C$^{\circ}$7

C7+ = C+7 = C7aug = C7$\sharp$5

C7sus4 = C11 = B$\flat$/C = Gm7/C

Cm$\sharp$7 = Cm(maj7) = C–Δ7 = CmΔ

Although chords are built in *root position* (root of chord in bass), notes may be moved up or down into other octaves to create a more pleasing sound. This is called a *voicing*. Here are four possibilities for a Cmaj7:

Cmaj7

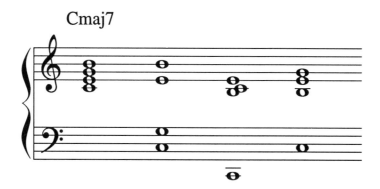

A chord that is voiced with a lowest note other than the root is said to be *inverted*. Inverting a chord does not change its basic sound, or its function.

In classical theory, inversions are considered significant; in jazz this is not so important—pianists, guitarists and bassists will make their own decisions about how to express chords. In fact, players often add notes that are not strictly called for in the basic chord, to add harmonic color. For example, a Cmaj7 chord might be voiced with an A, D, or F$\sharp$ added, or even with a G$\sharp$ replacing the G, if a performer desires that sound. Likewise, notes may be subtracted.

If a specific bass note is called for in an arrangement, it is indicated by a letter under a slash mark (e.g., "C7/E").

3. Seventh chords in major; Roman numeral notation

(examples: CD track 6)

To show all the seventh chords that naturally occur in a major key, we can stack up four-note chords from each scale tone, using only notes from that key. Each chord is assigned a Roman numeral, showing which scale step is the root:

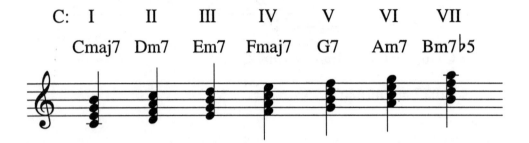

Because every major scale has the same interval structure, the resulting chord structures will also be the same in every major key. It will always be true that:

In any major key,

- I and IV are major 7 chords

- II, III, and VI are minor 7 chords

- V is dominant

- VII is minor 7♭5

The word *diatonic* refers to chords, or other scales, that are derived from the basic structure of a major scale. The seventh chords in major, above, are diatonic. Likewise, the natural minor scale and its chords are also diatonic.

This Roman numeral terminology gives us a way to describe and analyze chord structures. The example below shows a portion of a melody, with chord symbols, as you would see on a jazz "lead sheet." Above the music is a chordal analysis, showing the key we are in, and the Roman numerals that correspond to each chord.

In this book, we will assume that Roman numerals indicate seventh chords. In classical theory, plain Roman numerals refer to triads, with seventh chords shown as "V7" or "II7". You will see this notation in many jazz books, too.

4. Seventh chords in minor

Because minor has more than one form, and the form (natural, harmonic, or melodic) often changes within a piece, the type of chord found on a given scale step may vary.

But generally in a minor key,

- I is minor, minor 6, minor 7, or minor ♯7

- II is minor 7♭5

- III is not a common chord; it would be major 7.

- IV is minor, minor 6, or minor 7

- V is dominant ♭9, dom. ♯9, or *altered* (see Chapter 4, part 4)

- VI is major 7, often dominant

- VII is diminished (Bdim7) or dominant (B♭7)

5. Extensions and "avoid" notes *(examples: CD track 6)*

Ninths, elevenths, and thirteenths are often added to seventh chords to provide color. A ninth is like a second, but expressed as an upper chord tone. An eleventh is like a fourth, and a thirteenth is like a sixth.

These notes may be played as part of a melody or solo, or added to enrich a piano or guitar voicing. They are called *extensions*, *tension notes*, or *color tones*.

The most often-used extensions lie a whole step above the original chord tones. Extensions that lie a half step above the basic chord tones sound harsher, and are sometimes called *avoid notes*. This term is somewhat misleading—you do not actually need to avoid these notes at all; just be aware that the half-step relation introduces greater dissonance. (Exception: the ♭9, often added to V chords.)

Note that *any* interval, sounded against a chord, could be interpreted as a chord tone: root, ninth (= second), third, eleventh (= fourth), fifth, thirteenth (= sixth), or seventh.

The chords below are shown in root position, with each extension included in the chord's name.

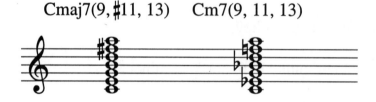

Cmaj7(9, ♯11, 13)   Cm7(9, 11, 13)

Sometimes a composer or arranger will specify exactly which extensions are to be played, as in the chord symbols above. More often, however, a jazz lead sheet will show a simpler chord name, with extensions (and voicings) left to the discretion of the performer. The chords above would probably be shown on a lead sheet as "Cmaj7(♯11)" and "Cm7." The pianist would add extensions as desired, and voice the chords as desired.

6. Polychords/upper structures *(examples: CD track 7)*

An extended chord is sometimes expressed as two simpler chords, one sounded above the other. Here are some useful possibilities:

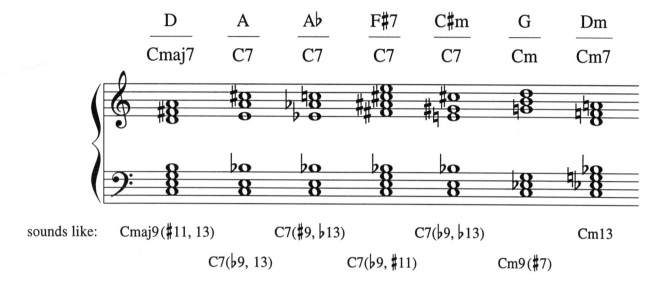

D	A	A♭	F♯7	C♯m	G	Dm
Cmaj7	C7	C7	C7	C7	Cm	Cm7

sounds like: Cmaj9(♯11, 13)   C7(♯9, ♭13)   C7(♭9, ♭13)   Cm13

            C7(♭9, 13)   C7(♭9, ♯11)   Cm9(♯7)

This *upper structure* or *polychord* concept can be useful in voicing chords or in soloing. If the upper chord is accentuated, its tones will sound like tension notes against the lower (basic) chord. At the same time, the upper structure will have a cohesion of its own.

If a specific polychord is intended in an arrangement, it will be shown as two chord symbols separated by a horizontal bar (as above), or by a slash (e.g., C/E7). Since "slash" notation could also indicate a specified bass note, you must consider the musical context to determine whether a polychord or a bass note is meant. Some arrangers reserve the horizontal line for indicating polychords.

Upper structures are often referred to by naming the position of the top chord's root, relative to the lower chord's root. For example, the first chord in the table above is an "upper structure II."

7. Exercises

- Build the following chords:

Abmaj7   Bbm7   E7   Bm7   Gm7b5   C#m7b5   Fdim7   F#7sus4

- Name the following chords:

- Finish the Roman numeral analysis for the following chord progression:

G: I

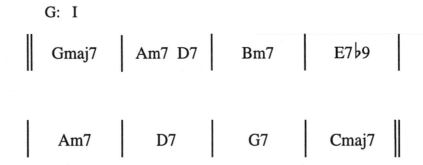

| Gmaj7 | Am7 D7 | Bm7 | E7b9 |

| Am7 | D7 | G7 | Cmaj7 |

- Play arpeggios for major 7 chords, as shown below. Move roots clockwise along the circle of fifths. Repeat this exercise for dominant, minor 7, minor 7b5, and diminished chords.

Cmaj7   Fmaj7   Bbmaj7   etc.

- Find a partner to quiz you. Example: "What is the IV chord in Eb major? Spell it." Or try this ear training exercise: One person plays a chord or arpeggio; the other tries to name its type.

Chapter 3

Chord Movement: Harmonic Clichés

Chords support melody not just with tonal color, but also by providing a sense of movement. In this chapter, we will consider some "harmonic clichés" that account for the vast majority of chord movements in jazz ("cliché" as used here carries no negative connotation). Most of these harmonic devices are found in traditional classical music as well.

You should learn to recognize these progressions by sound, as well as on paper. You can hear each example on the CD. Play them yourself, too, preferably on piano.

With each harmonic cliché are listed a few standard tunes that use it. Be sure to check out these tunes; most of them are readily available in fake books.

1. V to I *(examples: CD track 8)*

The most fundamental chord movement is from V to I.

The V chord (or "V7") produces a feeling of tension, moving to a feeling of rest with the I chord. This tension is caused by the fact that V contains an unstable interval, namely the d5 between the third and seventh. The d5 tries to resolve by moving along the half steps of the key, to the root and third of the I chord.

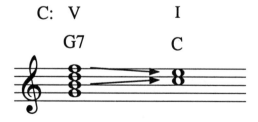

The listener feels a sense of satisfaction when the V resolves to the I. This motion is the basic harmonic driving force in virtually all Western music.

Remember that the only place a dominant seventh chord naturally occurs in a major key is on the V. This means that if you hear a dominant chord, your ear will probably pick it up as a V and expect a resolution to I. (An important exception is in blues, where I and IV could also be dominant.)

Applications to improvising:

- Since the basic force guiding harmony is the feeling of V (tension) to I (rest), your ideas will almost certainly follow the flow of tension and rest in the tune you are playing.

- If you emphasize the tonic note over the V chord (C over a G7 chord), you are sounding the "resolution" note over the tension chord—in a way, contradicting the flow of the progression.

  Also, the tonic (C) lies a half step above the third of the V chord (B), and thus is somewhat dissonant (a so-called "avoid" note—see Chapter 2, part 5).

- Because the V exists to produce tension, usually no harm is done by playing "tension" notes, or extensions (like ♯9 or ♭13), over the V. In fact, this only enhances the inherent tension of the V. To say that "anything goes" over the V is basically valid.

  The example below shows a possible solo line over a V to I progression, using the tensions ♭9 (A♭), ♯9 (B♭) and ♭13 (E♭) over the V chord. The V chord, as played under the line, could include these tensions, but this is not strictly necessary. You might note that this line relates to an upper structure E♭ triad, played over the G7 (see Chapter 2, part 6).

2. Circle of dominants *(examples: CD track 8)*

When a V resolves to its I, the chord roots move up a p4—for example, G7 to C. This is exactly the motion that you will see as you move clockwise along the circle of fifths (the same as "down a p5").

Chord roots moving in this way produce a strong, directional sound. If the chords are all dominant, we will hear a chain of resolutions, each V resolving into the next V. Here is an example of "circle of dominants" motion:

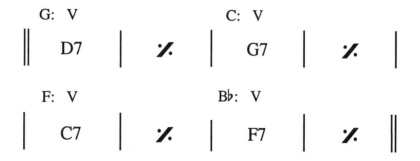

Among the countless standards that use this cliché, check out Don Redman's "Gee Baby, Ain't I Good to You," Duke Jordan's "Jordu," and the bridge (middle section) of "Rhythm changes" (see Chapter 6).

Application to improvising:

- If you track the thirds and sevenths of each chord in this progression, you will see that they form two lines that descend chromatically. These *guide tone lines* define the tones that drive the chord sequence. You may want to use the guide tones in a solo; in any case, you should always be aware of them.

 Here are the guide tone lines for the above example:

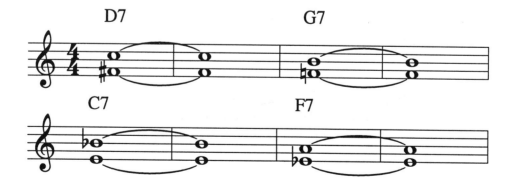

3. II V I *(examples: CD track 9)*

V to I (tension to release) is often prepared with the II chord (neutral-sounding), resulting in a II V I progression. This is a fundamental building block of jazz harmony.

II V I can be used as a phrase ending (*cadence*), or to establish a new key center. You will also often see II V, moving elsewhere, rather than resolving to I.

In a major key, II V I will look like*: m7 dom maj7*. In minor, it will look like: *m7b5 domb9 minor*. If you see one of these sequences, with roots moving along the circle, it will be a II V I.

Here is an example with two II V I sequences in major:

D: II	V	I	
Em7	A7	Dmaj7	℅

C: II	V	I	
Dm7	G7	Cmaj7	℅

Below is an example with three minor II V sequences, and a surprise resolution to major:

Dm: II	V	Cm: II	V
Em7b5	A7b9	Dm7b5	G7b9

Bbm: II	V	Bb: I	
Cm7b5	F7b9	Bbmaj7	℅

For other examples of II V I in major, see Joe Henderson's "No Me Esqueca," Clifford Brown's "Joy Spring," or David Raksin's "Laura." For minor II V examples, see Luis Bonfa's "Gentle Rain" or Thelonious Monk's "Round Midnight." Indeed, most jazz standards use this progression in some way. If you feel up for a little educational research, try to find standard tunes similar to the above examples!

Applications to improvising:

- A simple approach to improvising over a II V I is to use the single scale that contains all three chords. For example, over Gm7 C7 Fmaj7, you could use an F major scale. Although this technique is a bit limiting, it can be effective, if you use your ear.

- The active ingredient in a II V is the movement of the seventh of the II chord to the third (leading tone) of the V. For example, in Dm7 G7, the active tones are C to B. This is a "guide tone line," as mentioned in part 2 of this chapter. When you are learning to improvise on a tune, try using the guide tones.

- Because II V, or II V I, is such an essential building block, musicians often memorize melodic licks for soloing, or chord voicings for "comping" (i.e., accompanying), to fit the progression, practicing them in all 12 keys. For example,

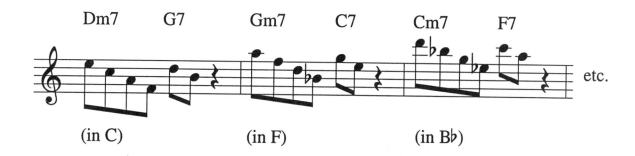

See Appendix A for some useful II V and II V I melodic patterns.

4. Circle of fifths within a key *(examples: CD track 9)*

If we move the chord roots by fourths, but use only notes naturally found in the key, we have the "circle of fifths within a key," also called the "diatonic circle of fifths." In Roman numerals, this cycle is:

I   IV   VII   III   VI   II   V   I

In C major, it works out to:

Cmaj7   Fmaj7   Bm7♭5   Em7   Am7   Dm7   G7   Cmaj7

Chord progressions often follow sections of this cycle. Note that the last three chords are II V I.

All the chord roots move by p4 except for the +4 interval between the IV and the VII. Often, one or more of the chords in this cycle will be made dominant.

Here is an example that uses the diatonic circle beginning on VI:

E♭: VI	II	V	I
Cm7	Fm7	B♭7	E♭maj7

IV	VII	V of VI	VI
A♭maj7	Dm7♭5	G7♭9	Cm7

For other examples in the standard repertoire, see Jerome Kern's "All the Things You Are," and Joseph Kosma's "Autumn Leaves." See also the bridges (middle sections) of Johnny Green's "Body and Soul," and Paul Desmond's "Take Five." And can you find the source of the above example? (Hint: It is often played in 3/4 time.)

Application to improvising:

- As with II V I, if you can identify a group of chords as belonging to a single scale, it opens up the possibility of simply improvising over the entire section with that single scale. Again, although this approach is easier, it is a bit limiting.

5. Deceptive cadences *(examples: CD track 10)*

In a deceptive cadence, V leads to some chord other than I. The target chord will usually contain some, but not all, the notes of the I.

The most common deceptive resolutions are to III and to VI. In the example below, the V chord in bar 4 resolves to the III chord in bar 5.

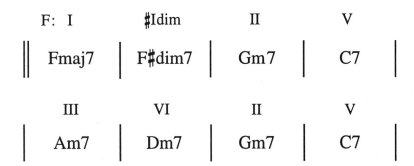

You can find examples in Thelonious Monk's "Round Midnight," Herbie Hancock's "Dolphin Dance," and Mal Waldron's "Soul Eyes," as well as the tune illustrated above.

Applications to improvising:

- If a V in major leads to the VI chord instead of I, you may wish to bring out the "relative minor" aspect of the VI, by playing an obviously minor lick over it.

- If the V leads to a III, you may wish to avoid the tonic note, since the intent of that progression is to avoid the resolution to I.

6. Common tones *(example: CD track 10)*

A chord change may sound smooth because the two chords have tones in common. The example below uses this device three times, in bars 4-5, 5-6, and 6-7.

Cm: I

Cm	Cm#7	Cm7	Cm6

VI	IV	II	V
Abmaj7	Fm7	Dm7b5	G7b9

For more examples of common-tone motion, see Antonio Carlos Jobim's "Once I Loved" (several instances), and the basic turnaround in part 11 of this chapter (I to VI).

Application to improvising:

- Chord substitutions are often made on the basis of common tones. You can use this concept in comping, soloing, or arranging. For example:

    Em7 might replace Cmaj7 (see "Deceptive cadences," part 5 of this chapter).

    Cmaj7 might replace Am7.

    Bm7b5 might replace G9. This substitution preserves the d5 interval B to F that drives the G7; it also keeps the A, for a "V in major" sound.

    Bdim7 might replace G7b9. This possibility is just like the above, but uses the note Ab, for a "V in minor" sound.

    C#m might replace C7(b9, b13). This substitution preserves the leading tone E and the notes C# (= Db) and G# (= Ab). You can find a nice example of this substitution in Antonio Carlos Jobim's "Dindi." This chord is one way to express "C7alt"; more on "alt" chords in Chapter 4, part 4.

    To see how "common tone" substitutions can relate to polychords, refer back to Chapter 2, part 6.

7. Secondary dominant *(example: CD track 11)*

Any chord may be prepared with its own V, thus focusing attention on, or "tonicizing", the target chord. In this example, there are secondary dominants in bars 2 and 5:

B♭: I		IV	III	V of II	II		D: II	V	
‖ B♭maj7	E♭maj7		Dm7	G7	Cm7	Cm7/B♭	Em7/A	A7	‖

B♭: III		V of VI	VI	subV of II	II		B♭m: II	V	
‖ Dm7	D7♯9		Gm7	D♭7	Cm7		Cm7♭5	F7♭9	‖

Secondary dominants are notated as "V of II" or "V of V"; you will also see "V/II" or "V(II)."

This is a very common device; you will see it in most standards. A few to look at are Duke Ellington's "Mood Indigo," Billy Strayhorn's "Take the 'A' Train," and Henry Mancini's "Days of Wine and Roses."

Secondary dominants are often prepared with their corresponding II chords, resulting in II V sequences. This occurs in measure 4, above.

In our 8-bar example, some musicians might argue that bar 2 is a II V in C major. Whether or not to consider this bar a key change to C major is a matter of personal opinion, based on how one hears the changes. As an improvising approach, either key (B♭ or C) could work as a set of notes to use over the Dm7.

Secondary dominants may also be used back-to-back, resulting in "circle of dominants" sequences (A7 D7 G7).

Application to improvising:

- When improvising over a secondary dominant, pay special attention to the third of the chord. It will usually be a "new note", not found in the basic key signature. In our 8-bar example, the G7 uses a B♮, and the D7♯9 uses an F♯.

8. Substitute dominant *(examples: CD track 11)*

Where a V would go, we may substitute a dominant chord built on the ♭2 scale step:

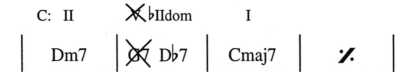

To see why this works, remember that the active tones in the G7 are B and F (third and seventh), resolving in the I chord to C and E. These same notes are present in the D♭7, as C♭ and F (seventh and third), and will resolve in the same way.

This substitution also provides a smooth, chromatic bass line when applied in a II V I (Dm7 D♭7 Cmaj7).

This device is called the "tritone substitution," because the roots of the V and ♭IIdom are a tritone (3 whole steps, or d5) apart, and because it exploits the tritone between third and seventh. The ♭IIdom chord is referred to as "sub V."

The tritone substitution is often used by performers where the composer originally wrote a V. It can work for the soloist even if the rhythm section is not using it, and vice versa.

Sometimes a composer will write the sub V into the tune, as in the following excerpt:

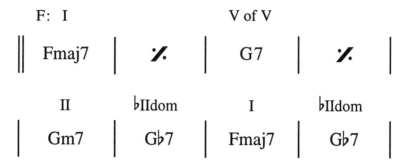

See also Dizzy Gillespie's "A Night in Tunisia" and Duke Ellington's "Satin Doll."

The tritone substitution can be used to turn a "circle of dominants" progression into a series of chromatically descending chords, as in the following example:

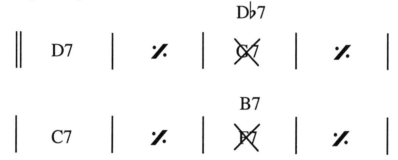

Applications to improvising:

- You can generally use this substitution in a solo, whether or not the rhythm section is doing so. Likewise, a rhythm section player can use it even if the soloist does not.

- You may want to work out some II ♭IIdom I patterns, in addition to your II V I ideas (see Appendix A).

- The tritone substitution usually works for any dominant chord that is acting as a V, including secondary dominants. Where a dominant chord is *not* acting as a V (for example, a IV chord in a blues progression), this substitution does not work.

9. Pivot Chords *(example: CD track 12)*

To move smoothly into a different key, composers often use *pivot chords*, chords that are naturally found in both the old and new keys. In the example below, Am7♭5 is approached as a VII in B♭, but then treated as a II in G minor.

B♭: II	V	I	IV
Cm7	F7	B♭maj7	E♭maj7

VII			
=Gm: II	V	I	B♭: V of II
Am7♭5	D7♭9	Gm7	G7♭9

The key change shown above, from major (B♭) to its relative minor, is one of the most common pivot chord modulations that you will encounter. See Harry Warren's "There Will Never Be Another You," or Victor Young's "Beautiful Love."

Some of the more cleverly designed progressions employ a sort of extended pivot chord concept, using chords that are plausible in the keys in question, but are not strictly diatonic members of the key. For example, see bars 5-7 of Jerome Kern's "All the Things You Are," where D♭maj7 is first presented as a IV in A♭, then treated as a sub V (although it is not dominant), pointed at the new key, C major.

Diminished 7 chords can be effective pivots. Because the chord tones are all separated by minor thirds, the root is ambiguous. In addition, this chord can either function as a VII replacing V (see Chapter 4, part 5) or as a passing chord. Composers may introduce a diminished chord one way, then treat it as though it has a different function. (See Antonio Carlos Jobim's "How Insensitive" and "Sabia.")

Application to improvising:

- Pivot chords belong to both the old and new keys in a modulation—however, in improvising, you have to decide which key is the one you wish to use. Although the *chord tones* may belong to both keys, the *scale* that is used over the chord may differ somewhat, depending on which key center you consider more relevant.

10. IVm and ♭VIIdom, modal interchange *(example: CD track 12)*

This device is used to add minor color to a piece that is basically in major; we might think of it as a standard device in major. Here is an example :

C: I		IVm ♭VIIdom		I subV of VI		V of II	
‖ C6		Fm7 B♭7		C6 B♭7		A7	

Although the Fm7 B♭7 looks like a II V in E♭, the ear will not perceive E♭ as tonic. Instead, the ear retains C as tonic, interpreting Fm7 B♭7 as a temporary shift to C *minor*, where they are normal IV and VII chords. The active ingredient in establishing this feeling of minor is the ♭6 of the key (A♭, in the key of C).

This shift from major to parallel minor (C major to C minor) is called *modal interchange*. The IVm and ♭VIIdom chord are *borrowed chords* from the parallel minor. Chords that suggest minor by including the ♭6 form a group called *subdominant minor* chords.

Sometimes the minor color introduced by this device only consists of the ♭6 note. For example, an Fm♯7 chord in a C major tune would introduce both the A♭ and an E♮. The E♮ certainly means that this is less than a shift to C minor; but the A♭ still provides minor color.

You might see the IVm and ♭VIIdom used singly or together; they serve the same function. Sometimes the ♭VIIdom used where a V would go, as a different sort of substitute dominant (see Antonio Carlos Jobim's "Meditation," and the bridge to Kurt Weill's "Speak Low").

The IVm often appears as part of the sequence IV IVm I (Fmaj7 Fm6 Cmaj7) or IV IVm III . This progression sets up a strong guide tone line, with the notes A to A♭ to G (see Jerome Kern's "All the Things You Are," John Klenner's "Just Friends," or Hoagy Carmichael's "Stardust").

Subdominant minor chords are found in many standards. Besides those listed above, check out Thad Jones' "A Child is Born" and Cole Porter's "All of You."

Modal interchange in a minor-key piece (using chords borrowed from major) is also possible, though less commonly seen.

Applications to improvising:

- The note that drives all of the subdominant minor chords is the ♭6 of the key (A♭, in the key of C). Explore this note when learning to solo on a tune with this harmonic device.

- One subdominant minor chord can often substitute for another. For example, IVm might be replaced by ♭VIIdom. The same licks and scales will usually fit either chord.

11. Turnarounds, tags, vamps *(examples: CD track 13)*

Turnarounds are used at the end of a tune, or the end of a section, to set up a return to the beginning. A turnaround usually consists of four chords in two measures, two beats for each chord, involving some variation of I VI II V. Note that this is the last part of the "circle within a key."

A few standard turnarounds are listed below; they all derive from I VI II V, with variations coming from secondary dominants or substitute dominants. These turnarounds are shown in C; look at them in Roman numeral terms.

Cmaj7	Am7	Dm7	G7	
Cmaj7	A7	Dm7	G7	
Cmaj7	C#dim7	Dm7	G7	
Em7	E♭7	Dm7	D♭7	
Em7	E♭7	D7	D♭7	
Em7♭5	A7♭9	Dm7♭5	G7♭9	
Cmaj7	E♭7	A♭maj7	D♭7	

The last turnaround shown above (sometimes played with all major 7 chords) is often referred to as a "Lady Bird" turnaround, because it is used in Tadd Dameron's tune of that name. See also Wes Montgomery's "West Coast Blues," and Miles Davis' "Half Nelson."

A *tag* is a standard way to end an arrangement; usually it consists of the last four measures of a tune, repeated one or two more times. When the last four bars are the very common II V I ℀ (one bar each), often the tag will be set up by playing V of II instead of the final I chord. For example, in a tune that normally ends Dm7 G7 Cmaj7 ℀ , our tag would go: Dm7 G7 Cmaj7 A7♭9 , repeated, then finishing Dm7 G7 Cmaj7 ℀ .

Some tunes include built-in tags as part of the basic progression. For example, see Antonio Carlos Jobim's "Corcovado," or Harold Arlen's "Stormy Weather."

A *vamp* is a repeating chord progression, often used as an introduction, interlude, or ending, especially in Latin American styles (Afro-Cuban vamps are often called *montunos*). Here are three common vamps:

|| Cmaj7 | D♭7 | Cmaj7 | D♭7 | etc.

|| C7 | B♭7 | C7 | B♭7 | etc.

|| Dm7 | G7 | Dm7 | G7 | etc.

This last vamp looks like a II V in C major, but really is a I to IV progression in D dorian (similar to D minor; more about this in Chapter 4).

Vamps similar to the three above occur in Jobim's "Girl From Ipanema," "Wave," and "Triste," Benny Golson's "Killer Joe," and Tito Puente's "Oye Como Va."

Application to improvising:

- As with II V patterns, many players practice melodic patterns or chord voicings for standard turnarounds, in 12 keys. For example:

12. Exercises

- Identify the standards that use chord progressions closely resembling the unidentified examples in this chapter.

- Pick a tune to learn. Use any of the tunes mentioned in this chapter, or another tune of your choice. Find a good lead sheet, and:

    (a) Memorize the melody (chord changes too, if possible).

    (b) Photocopy the lead sheet or copy out the chords, and write a harmonic analysis above the chords, noting the key centers.

    (c) On a separate sheet of paper, list as many harmonic clichés as you can, noting where they occur by measure numbers.

    (d) Practice improvising on the tune. Step one: embellish the melody. Step two: diverge further and further from the melody, while observing the key centers. Step three: ignore the original melody, and play your own lines over the chords. Keep to the key centers, and try to include "strong notes," such as the third of all secondary dominants, the ♭3 of all IVm chords, and the seventh of all ♭VIIdom chords.

    (e) Transpose the tune (basic melody and chords) to some other key. Practice improvising, as above, in the new key.

- Repeat this process with other tunes.

Chapter 4

Modes and Chord Scales

In contemporary jazz theory, every chord has one or more scales that can be played over it. Players use these scales as raw material for soloing—not necessarily as scalar runs, but as sets of notes that are compatible with the chords.

The chord scale system in common use today consists of the seven *modes of major*, seven *modes of melodic minor*, *diminished* scales, and *whole tone* scales. This group will provide a scale to fit virtually any chord (see Appendix B for the logic behind this system).

In this chapter, we will discuss these scales, as well as two other scale types often used by modern players, *bebop* and *pentatonic* scales.

1. Scale tones as chord extensions *(example: CD track 14)*

The following example shows a C7♯11 chord in root position, with added tensions 9 and 13 (often included in dominant ♯11 chords). The corresponding scale is "C lydian dominant."

Notice this important point: *Every note in the scale could be regarded as a chord tone*. The chord lays out the notes vertically, the scale lays them out horizontally.

C7♯11   C lydian dominant

2. Modes of major *(examples: CD track 14)*

The modes of major are a group of scales that can be derived from the basic major scale pattern, by using different starting notes. For example, if we use the notes of C major, but treat D as the tonic, we have generated a "dorian" scale, with half steps between 2-3 and 6-7.

Each mode is identified with a Greek name; in this scheme, major (ionian) and natural minor (aeolian) also have Greek names. Each mode has a characteristic pattern of whole and half steps, and thus its own unique sound.

Modes are used in ways that may, or may not, relate to the "parent" scale. For example, a D dorian scale can be used to improvise over a II chord in C major (Dm7). On the other hand, D dorian might be used as a tonality in itself, with D the tonic note. Miles Davis' "So What" is in the key of D dorian, and really has nothing to do with the key of C major.

Below are the modes of major, shown first as derived from C major, then built from the note C, using the appropriate whole/half pattern. Also listed are how the mode's structure compares to major or natural minor, and the chord type over which the mode may be played.

ionian (major):

1 to 1 of major; half steps 3-4 and 7-8. Fits major 7 chords (usually I in major).

dorian:

2 to 2 of major; half steps 2-3 and 6-7; like major with ♭3 and ♭7, or like natural minor with a major 6. Fits minor 7 chords (usually II in major, or I in dorian).

phrygian:

3 to 3 of major; half steps 1-2 and 5-6; like major with ♭2, ♭3, ♭6, ♭7, or like natural minor with ♭2; "Spanish" sound. Fits minor 7 chords (when found as III in major, or I in phrygian).

lydian:

4 to 4 of major; half steps 4-5 and 7-8; like major with ♯4. Fits major 7 chords (when used as IV in major, or as I in lydian; sometimes used over I in major).

mixolydian:

5 to 5 of major; half steps 3-4 and 6-7; like major with ♭7. Fits dominant 7 chords (V in major, also I and IV in blues). Sometimes called the *dominant scale*.

aeolian (natural minor):

6 to 6 of major; half steps 2-3 and 5-6; same as natural minor, or like major with ♭3, ♭6, ♭7. Fits minor 7 chords (when used as VI in major, or I in minor).

locrian:

7 to 7 of major; half steps 1-2 and 4-5; like major with ♭2, ♭3, ♭5, ♭6, ♭7, or natural minor with ♭2, ♭5. Fits minor 7 ♭5 chords (usually II in minor, occasionally VII or ♯IV in major).

3. Modes of major, continued

The strong or defining notes of each mode are the notes that create its distinctive sound. The dorian note is M6; phrygian is ♭2; lydian is ♯4; mixolydian is ♭7; aeolian is ♭6; locrian is ♭5.

The modes are sometimes thought of as "bright" to "dark": lydian, ionian, mixolydian, dorian, aeolian, phrygian, locrian.

4. Modes of melodic minor *(examples: CD track 15)*

Another set of interesting and useful scales is formed by the modes of melodic minor. (In jazz theory, the term "melodic minor" refers only to the ascending half of the classical melodic minor scale.)

As with major, these modes are not necessarily functionally connected to the "parent" scale—we are using major and melodic minor only as interval patterns from which to generate the modes. Once we derive these new scales, they are unique tonalities in themselves.

The modes of melodic minor are shown below.

melodic minor:

1-1 of melodic minor; half steps 2-3 and 7-8; like major with ♭3. Fits minor 6 or minor ♯7 chords (usually I or IV in minor).

dorian ♭2:

2 to 2 of melodic minor; half steps 1-2 and 6-7. Fits sus4 ♭9 chords (sometimes seen as V in minor). Not used much.

lydian augmented:

3 to 3 of melodic minor; like major with ♯4 and ♯5. Fits major 7 ♯5 chords (sometimes seen as I). In some jazz theory methods, this is considered the basic scale for generating the melodic minor group.

lydian dominant:

4 to 4 of melodic minor; like major with #4 and ♭7. Fits dominant #11 chords (often seen as V of V, as ♭IIdom, or as ♭VIIdom).

mixolydian ♭6:

5 to 5 of melodic minor; half steps 3-4 and 5-6; like major with ♭6 and ♭7; could fit dominant (9, ♭13). Not used much.

locrian #2:

6 to 6 of melodic minor; half steps 2-3 and 4-5; like natural minor with ♭5.
Fits minor 7 ♭5 chords (usually encountered as II in minor).

altered ("alt"):

7 to 7 of melodic minor; like natural minor with ♭2, ♭4, and ♭5; fits "alt" chords
(V in minor, but often encountered as V in an otherwise major context).
Also called *diminished whole tone, or superlocrian.*

"alt" is a general term for a dominant chord that is colored with a ♭9, #9, ♭5
(= #11), and/or #5 (= ♭13). In other words, both ninth and fifth are altered.
The chord can thus actually be played in several different ways (most
commonly with #9, ♭13). The scale contains all these alterations, plus the root,
M3, and ♭7 of the chord. It may be used over any form of the "alt" chord.
(You may notice that our examples contain some enharmonic "misspellings.")

5. Whole tone and diminished scales *(examples: CD track 16)*

The *whole tone* scale is built with six notes, arranged in consecutive whole steps. This scale, like the *chromatic* scale (all half steps) and the *diminished* scale (alternating whole and half steps), is a *symmetrical* scale.

The whole tone scale is useful in improvising over augmented triads and dominant (♯5, 9) chords. It has a rootless, floating feeling, due to its symmetrical structure (whole tone passages have often been used by movie score composers for "dream" music).

There are only two whole tone scales: the one that starts at the bottom of your instrument, and the one that starts a half step higher.

C (or D, E, F♯, G♯, B♭) whole tone

C♯ (or D♯, F, G, A, B) whole tone

The *diminished* scale is shown below. As with the whole tone scale, the root is ambiguous. There are exactly three diminished scales, each with four possible roots.

C (or E♭, F♯, A) diminished

fits: Cdim7

C♯ (or E, G, B♭) diminished

fits: C♯dim7

D (or F, A♭, B) diminished

fits: Ddim7

The diminished scale is often used for improvising over diminished chords (it consists only of chord tones, and tension notes a whole step above each chord tone).

Another important use is over dominant ♭9 chords (start the scale on the ♭9, beginning with a whole step). This works because a dominant ♭9 chord equals a diminished chord, if the dominant chord is voiced with the ♭9 replacing the root.

C7♭9 = C♯dim7, so use C♯ dim. scale

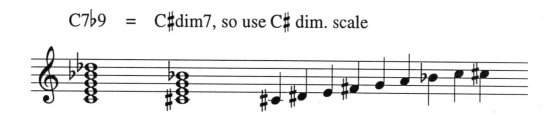

If the dominant ♭9 chord includes or implies a major 13, use this scale. For dominant (♭9, ♭13), the altered scale is used, starting from the chord root.

6. Bebop scales *(examples: CD track 17)*

Though they are not part of the basic group of scales listed above, *bebop* scales are a concept that you should be aware of. A bebop scale is a seven-note mode with one chromatic passing tone added (David Baker, a renowned jazz educator, coined this term to describe a practice often used by the classic bop improvisers).

C bebop dominant

fits: C7

C bebop major

fits: Cmaj7

The added note allows the scale to be played over a corresponding dominant chord, with chord tones occurring on the accented beats:

C7

Adding chromatic tones to make a phrase "scan" is not an idea unique to jazz; it is found throughout the history of Western music. Include bebop scales in your practice routine—it will help you apply the added chromatic tones in your playing.

7. Pentatonic scales *(examples: CD track 17)*

The term *pentatonic* ("five notes") has been used to describe a variety
of five-note scales; the most commonly used are *major pentatonic* and
minor pentatonic:

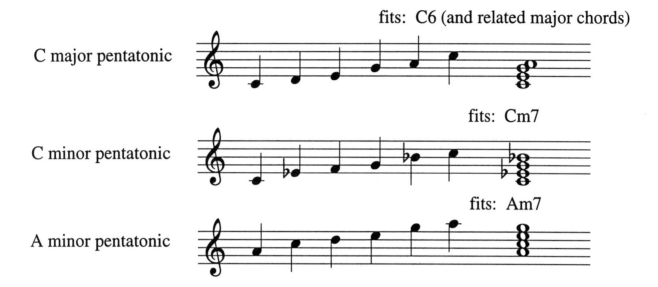

Major pentatonic relates to minor pentatonic in exactly the same way that
major relates to its relative minor (same notes, different roots—compare
the C major and A minor pentatonic scales, above).

Just as bebop scales are "added note" scales, derived from seven-note modes,
pentatonic scales are like major and minor scales with notes subtracted.

These scales sound a little less predictable than traditional scales made up of
major seconds and minor seconds. Here the minor seconds have been
eliminated, and two minor thirds result. Pentatonic scale patterns can have a
"bluesy" tinge; in fact, you should note that minor pentatonic needs only a
♯4 to become a blues scale.

Players using a pentatonic approach will often play four-note groups at
quick tempos (this has become a "modern" cliché). For example:

etc.

8. Exercises

- Play the following modes, all with C as the root, for one octave, up and down (one note will change for each successive scale): major, lydian, lydian dominant, mixolydian, dorian, natural minor, phrygian, locrian, altered.

- Repeat with F as root, then B♭, etc., around the circle of fifths.

- Practice (and memorize) all the scales mentioned in this chapter. Obviously, this is a long-term project, but you should start on it immediately.

- Practice improvising with each mode. Try a different mode, and a different root, each day.

- Take a lead sheet for any standard tune you have previously analyzed, and note next to each chord symbol the scale (or scales) that could fit it.

Chapter 5

Blues

Blues is a musical tradition that has been closely tied to jazz since the origins of both idioms in the late 1800s. The melodic ideas and expressive techniques of blues are essential to jazz. You must be comfortable and fluent with blues; most players know plenty of blues melodies and phrases. Blues influences are found in all styles of jazz and American popular music: dixieland, swing, bebop, funk, folk, R&B, heavy metal, country, free jazz, hip-hop, etc.

You can practice improvising with the play-along track on the CD *(CD track 22)*, which features a rhythm section playing three choruses of slow blues in concert F. Chord charts for the play-along tracks are in Appendix C; the sample solo in part 8 uses the same chord progression.

1. Blue notes and the blues scale *(example: CD track 18)*

Blue notes are the ♭3, ♭5, and ♭7 of the key; blues music uses these notes in ways not found in classical music.

The *blues scale*, incorporating the blue notes, is often used as a source of ideas for blues solos, and as a starting point for beginning improvisers. Various "blues scales" have been suggested over the years; below is the most widely accepted version.

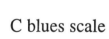

This scale, if used with good taste, can be used to improvise over the entire 12 bars of a basic blues progression. Important note: the blues scale is a relatively recent idea, dating from about the 1930s, and there are plenty of traditional licks that don't fit this scale.

2. Basic blues progression *(examples: CD track 18)*

In theory terms, "blues" is a musical *form* with a particular 12-measure chord sequence, always some variation of the following:

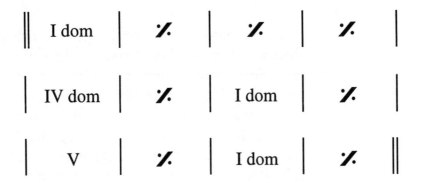

Here is how the basic blues progression works out in the key of C:

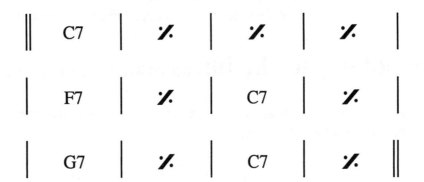

Although this is the framework common to virtually all blues tunes, you will not often hear a blues played in this simple form, particularly in a jazz context. On the next page is one of the more basic forms you may encounter; later in this chapter we will explore the ways that jazz players generally interpret blues changes.

The basic progression is usually filled out by the addition of IV dom and V chords in bars 2, 10, and 12, as follows:

The G7 in bar 12 sets up the return to the top of the progression, and would be omitted at the end of the tune.

In slow blues, bars 11 and 12 often include the following turnaround:

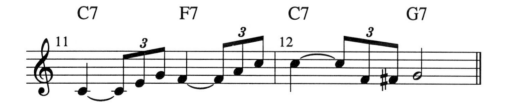

Here is a classic lick that might be played over this turnaround:

59

3. Dominant I and IV *(examples: CD track 19)*

In traditional European music, V is normally the only dominant chord. The use of dominant I and IV chords is unique to blues, and carries special implications.

Blues has roots in both European and African music. One significant African element is the lowered ("flat") seventh; many melodic phrases associated with jazz, rock, and blues use the ♭7. These phrases are are naturally harmonized with dominant I and IV chords. For example,

When the I chord is dominant (C7), it functions also as V of IV (C7 is V of F), setting up a strong movement into the IV chord (F7) in the fifth measure. This is an important structural element of blues.

Adding tension notes to the I, particularly in the fourth bar, makes the I sound even more like a V of IV. This can be done by the chording instruments, or in the solo line (first example below). Simply accentuating the ♭7 in bar 4 can produce the same effect (second example).

4. Variable third *(example: CD track 19)*

When the IV chord is dominant (F7, in the key of C), it introduces a new note into the overall tonality: the seventh of the chord (E♭), which is the ♭3 of the key.

An important thread running through the blues is the movement of the third of the key from major to minor (E and E♭, in a C blues), as it occurs in the I and IV chords. You should be aware of this tonal element when improvising. The melodies of many blues tunes include this "thread" (see W. C. Handy's "St. Louis Blues" and Sonny Rollins' "Tenor Madness").

This "thread" (actually a guide tone line) is shown below, as it occurs in a C blues.

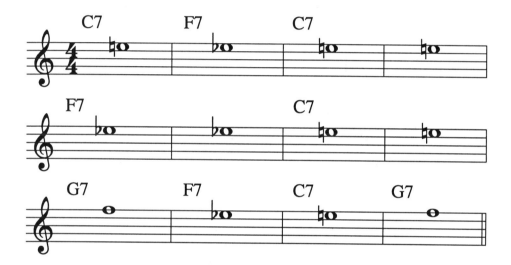

A blues scale can be used for improvising over the whole 12 bars of a blues. Note that it uses only the minor third. The minor third sounds all right when played over the major third in the I chord, but the *major* third (E, in a C blues) doesn't work very well over the IV chord, which includes the ♭3 of the key (E♭). After learning to use the blues scale, beginning students should learn where the major third works in a blues solo. (See the sample solo in part 8 of this chapter.)

The motion of this line, as well as the acceptability of playing a minor third against a chord with a major third, is related to a traditional practice of bending the pitch of melody notes.

5. Bebop blues *(examples: CD track 20)*

There are many variations of the basic blues progression; below is a version that has been standard in jazz since the 1940s. In addition to the elements we have used so far, this progression includes: a II V in bar 4; a passing diminished chord in bar 6; a V of II in bar 8; a II V in bars 9 and 10; and a two-bar turnaround. Similar progressions are used for Charlie Parker's "Now's the Time" and "Billie's Bounce," and Sonny Rollins' "Tenor Madness," as well as countless other bop-style blues tunes.

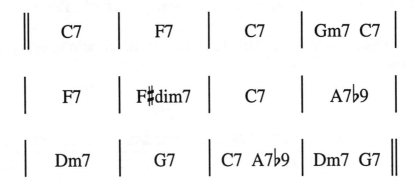

In this variation, soloists frequently define the V of II in bar 8 by sounding the third of the chord (C♯, in this example), or by arpeggiating the chord. It is a bop soloist's cliché to arpeggiate this chord up from the 3 to the ♭9.

When a jazz group performs a blues, the players do not necessarily stick to one exact progression, but rather use standard alterations, as they see fit, often without discussing it beforehand. If the players keep alert, this does not present a problem. In actual performance, you may encounter any of the blues variations in this chapter, combined in various ways.

In addition to the progressions in this chapter, variations may involve using the sub V (see Chapter 3, part 8) or different turnarounds (Chapter 3, part 11).

6. Minor blues *(example: CD track 20)*

Some blues tunes follow a 12-bar progression in a minor key. Often the I and IV will be minor 7 chords; a dorian scale will fit each. The V may be minor (dorian) also, leading to a generally modal feeling, or it may be dominant.

Here is a common version of minor blues:

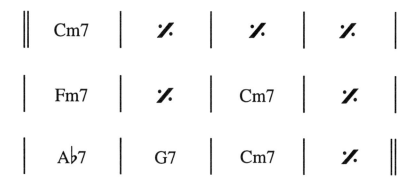

(See John Coltrane's "Equinox" and "Mr. P. C.")

In a minor blues, a dominant V chord presents several possibilities for a corresponding scale, depending on which tension notes you wish to imply. If you are playing a C minor blues, some possibilities for the G7 include:

- A♭ diminished—implies G7(♭9, 13)

- C harmonic minor—implies G7(♭9, ♭13)

- G alt—implies G7(♯9, ♭13), or any other "alt" variation

- C blues scale—implies G7(♯9, ♭13), but use your ear, as some notes can clash.

For a scale to use over the A♭7, try the C blues scale (this is an opportunity to use licks with the ♭5 note, G♭), A♭ lydian dominant, or A diminished.

7. "Bird blues" and other variations *(example: CD track 20)*

Below is a progression created by Charlie Parker, expanding on bop blues. It has two distinctive features: the use of a major 7 chord for the I, and the addition of II V sequences in bars 2, 3, 6, 7, and 8. This progression gives the soloist a more interesting and challenging chordal basis to work with, while preserving the basic harmonic landmarks of blues in bars 1, 5, and 10-12.

Cmaj7	Bm7♭5 E7♭9	Am7 D7	Gm7 C7
F7	Fm7 B♭7	Em7 A7	E♭m7 A♭7
Dm7	G7	C7 A7♭9	Dm7 G7

Chord changes similar to these are found in Parker's "Blues for Alice" and in Wes Montgomery's "West Coast Blues," as well as in several non-blues standards. For example, compare Toots Thielmann's "Bluesette," Parker's "Confirmation," and Harry Warren's "There Will Never Be Another You."

A tune can project a blues feeling in ways other than the 12-bar progression. The form may be extended or altered (as in Herbie Hancock's "Watermelon Man"). Some tunes preserve only 12-bar length, or the feeling of a chord change in the fifth measure (see Charles Mingus' "Nostalgia in Times Square"). Or the chord structure may be completely different, with a bluesy feeling conveyed melodically and/or rhythmically (Duke Ellington's "It Don't Mean a Thing," Freddie Hubbard's "Mr. Clean," Ornette Coleman's "Blues Connotation").

8. Sample solo *(example: CD track 21; Blues in F play-along: CD track 22)*

Play through the following solo—two choruses of slow blues in F, with bop-style changes. Note that chords and scales are only background concepts; the basic building blocks are really licks and motives (rhythmic/melodic shapes). If a lick sounds good to you, extract it and practice it in 12 keys. Transpositions for B♭ and E♭ instruments can be found in Appendix C.

The play-along track uses the same changes as the sample solo. You will find chord charts for C, B♭ and E♭ instruments in Appendix C also.

9. Exercises

- Memorize blues scales in all 12 keys. Practice soloing in each key.

- Write out the chord changes for bebop-style blues, in all 12 keys.

- Compose a blues melody in C, using a four-bar riff repeated three times (example shown below). If your melody uses an E (the major third), you may want to change that note to E♭ when it occurs over the F7 chord. (See Duke Ellington's "Duke's Place," Count Basie's "One O'clock Jump," Woody Herman's "Woodchopper's Ball," Charlie Parker's "Cool Blues," and Milt Jackson's "Bags' Groove," among the countless examples of riff blues.)

- Compose a head to fit a "Bird blues" progression in F.

- Although you should be ready to play blues in any key, in reality some keys are used more often than others. Make sure that you are comfortable soloing over bop-style blues in B♭, F and C; basic blues in E (a favorite key for rock guitarists—use the last version in part 2 of this chapter); Bird blues in F; minor blues in C minor.

- Practice soloing unaccompanied; try to hear the changes in your head. If this is difficult, outline the chords with your solo line.

- Practice blues soloing with your voice. Use "scat" syllables, or a neutral syllable, or whistle or hum.

- Practice blues soloing in your head, without an instrument. Imagine the fingerings on your instrument.

Chapter 6

Rhythm Changes

Rhythm changes are another standard chord progression that, like blues, has served to harmonize countless melodies. When you study Rhythm changes, you are simultaneously learning "Anthropology," "Dexterity," "Steeplechase," "Oleo," and many more (see Chapter 8, part 5, for more Rhythm tunes).

The practice of using this harmonic framework began in the 1930s, and became extremely common in the 1940s and 1950s. Today, this progression is a basic subject in the education of every jazz musician.

You will find a play-along track with three choruses of Rhythm changes in B♭ on the CD *(CD track 26)*.

1. Chord chart and analysis *(example: CD track 23)*

Rhythm changes are played with many variations; the progression shown on the following page represents a version that most jazz musicians regard as basic. Although a George Gershwin tune was the historical origin of this progression, the changes shown here are not Gershwin's. The original changes were geared to supporting the original melody, including a two-bar tag that is virtually always eliminated in later Rhythm tunes. The progression shown here is the result of years of modification by performers, who arrived at changes better suited for improvising.

As with blues, and jazz in general, musicians frequently alter the changes even further in performance, often on the spur of the moment. In part 3 of this chapter we will discuss some standard variations.

Rhythm changes are most often encountered in the key of B♭, as shown. (The slash marks indicate beats. They are not meant to indicate a comping rhythm; that is up to the performer.)

67

Rhythm changes

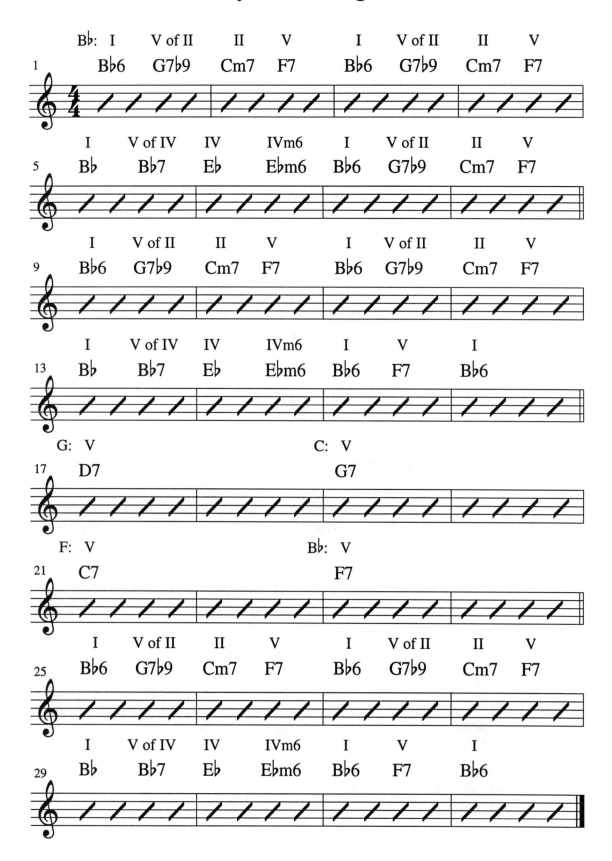

Here is an overview of the chord progression:

First A section (measures 1-8):

- Measures 1-2 consist of a two-bar turnaround, repeated in bars 3-4.

- In measure 5, the I chord becomes dominant, turning it into a V of IV. It resolves to the IV in bar 6, moving to IV minor on beat 3 of that measure.

- Measures 7-8 are another two-bar turnaround.

Second A section (measures 9-16):

- When the A section repeats, the only difference is in bars 15-16, where a I V I cadence replaces the turnaround.

B section, or "bridge" (measures 17-24):

- The B section consists of dominant chords, two bars each, moving around the circle of fifths. The bridge begins on D7 (III dominant in the key of B♭, or V in G), with each chord resolving into the next, finishing on F7 (V in B♭), which sets up the return to the last A section. This bridge is an example of the "circle of dominants" harmonic cliché.

Third A section (measures 25-32):

- In order to set up the return to the top of the progression, the last two bars are usually played with a turnaround, as in measures 7-8. When ending the tune, the final A section is exactly like the second A.

2. Improvising on Rhythm changes *(example: CD track 24)*

Rhythm tunes are often taken at rapid tempos, making it difficult to gear your improvising to each chord. But there are some shortcuts that can make your creative task much easier. Below are some approaches that may help.

On the simplest level, you could stick entirely to the key of B♭ major for the A sections, and use mixolydian scales for each of the chords in the bridge. This approach is a little simplistic, but will work, on a basic level.

For a little more interest in the A sections, try using B♭ major over bars 1-4, and blues ideas over bars 5-8. Better yet, a mixture of blues and major scale ideas can work well over the entire A section, if you use your ear. (See the sample solo in part 4 of this chapter, bars 2, 9-12, 15-16, and 24.)

Since the A sections contain several two-bar turnarounds, another common approach is to think in terms of turnaround patterns. Likewise, II V patterns can be used where appropriate. (Sample solo, bars 3-4, 25-26, and 27-28.)

Bars 5-7 contain a strong guide tone line that can serve as a framework for embellishment. Note that this line includes the ♭7 of the I dom (V of IV), and the ♭3 of the IVm chord. These are "new" notes that strongly define the harmonic motion:

(See the sample solo, bars 5-7).

The bridge presents some interesting possibilities. One alternative is to treat each chord as a separate tonal center, with a dominant I chord, as in a blues, and play blues licks (with major or minor third) over each chord.

Another approach for the bridge is to treat each chord as a V, and enhance its unstable quality by using scales or licks that contain altered tensions. (Sample solo, bars 17-24).

For a soloing approach with more harmonic complexity, try using some of the substitutions covered in part 3, which follows.

3. Variations on the progression *(examples: CD track 24)*

Soloists and/or rhythm section players often alter the progression, with or without informing the rest of the band (this often happens in jazz). A few often-used variations are listed below:

Variations for the A section:

- The two-bar turnarounds may be altered in any of the ways shown in Chapter 3, part 11. For example, the first 4 bars could be:

‖ Bb6   Bdim7 | Cm7   F7 ‖ Dm7   Db7 | Cm7   B7 |

or

‖ Bbmaj7 Gm7 | Gb7   F7 | Bb6   Db7 | C7   B7 |

- The IVm in bar 6 may be replaced by a bVIIdom (see Chapter 3, part 10), or by a #IVdim. The guide tone line works over these chords, too. Bars 5-8 could be:

| Bb   Bb7 | Eb6   Ab7 | Dm7   G7b9 | Cm7   F7 ‖

or

| Bb   Bb7 | Eb6 Edim7 | Bb6   Db7 | C7   B7 ‖

- In some compositions, a different progression may be used for the A section, keeping the "Rhythm bridge" changes (e.g., Parker's "Scrapple from the Apple," or Duke Ellington's "Perdido"). This progression becomes part of the new tune, not a "spur of the moment" variation.

Variations for the bridge:

- Tritone substitutions may be used in bars 19-20 and 23-24, creating a series of chromatically descending chords:

‖ D7		⁒		D♭7		⁒	
	C7		⁒		B7		⁒ ‖

- Each two-bar dominant chord may be replaced by a II V :

‖ Am7	D7	Dm7	G7
Gm7	C7	Cm7	F7 ‖

- A different bridge may be used, keeping Rhythm changes for the A section (e.g., Tadd Dameron's "Good Bait"). As before, this progression is a basis for the new tune, not a variation to be used in performing a regular "Rhythm" tune.

4. Sample solo *(example: CD track 25; Rhythm changes play-along: CD track 26)*

Play through the following solo. Features to check:

- The rhythmic pattern in bar 1 is a recurring motif.

- The guide tone line is embellished in measures 5-7.

- Turnaround patterns in bars 3-4, 25-26, and 27-28.

- Melodic development by sequencing—e.g., measures 5-7 and 9-11.

- Blues ideas are used whether or not they "theoretically" fit the chord.

- Some fairly "out" or polytonal ideas in measures 16-23.

You will find B♭ and E♭ transpositions for this solo in Appendix C. The play-along track uses the same changes; see Appendix C for chord charts.

5. Exercises

- Memorize several heads for Rhythm changes. See Chapter 8, part 5, for a list of some of the best-known Rhythm tunes.

- Transpose one or two of these melodies into some other key—preferably by ear, not on paper.

- Practice soloing unaccompanied over Rhythm changes in B♭ concert (most Rhythm tunes are in this key). Outline the changes enough to define them for a listener.

- Listen to some of the classic recordings of Rhythm tunes by players like Charlie Parker and Sonny Rollins. Transcribe solos, or parts of them. As a starting point, check out any of Parker's "Anthropology" recordings. For a terrific already-transcribed solo, see the "Anthropology" improvisation that appears in the *Charlie Parker Omnibook* (see the Bibliography, Appendix D).

- Write a Rhythm tune. The easy way: Write an 8-measure A section, use it over each A in the progression, and assume the bridge will be improvised. More ambitious: Include a composed bridge. Even more ambitious: Do not repeat A sections, but rather write a continuous "through-composed" melody over the entire progression. Most ambitious: Rewrite the chord progression, with substitutions, and write a corresponding head (melody).

Chapter 7

Approaches to Improvising

It is a good idea to keep things in proper perspective—theory is just one small aspect of jazz improvisation.

We study theory to improve our understanding of *sound*; our real goal is to improve our ability to work creatively with sound.

In this chapter, we will discuss some important aspects of improvising that are not considered in the harmonic/melodic system that we have studied so far.

1. Beyond theory *(example: CD track 27)*

Where did this lick come from? Does it derive from a C7 chord, from a C mixolydian scale, or maybe from a C blues scale?

It doesn't matter. The best answer might be that it is a traditional lick, related to all of these concepts.

Most jazz musicians begin their educational process by copying licks from recordings of players whom they respect. Theory really is secondary to "learning the language." As a player gains experience, he or she evolves a personal style.

But learning licks, like knowing theory, is not really the point, either. The objective of all this educational preparation is to enrich your personal resources, so that your creativity has the best possible tools to work with.

When you perform, all your theory training should recede to the background. Play from your own sense of expression and continuity. Play by ear. Try to get beyond theory.

Here are some points of advice, that have little to do with theory:

- Everything you play should mean something. What are you trying to say in your solo?

- Don't just improvise with notes; don't just improvise with phrases. Use texture, emotion, volume, tone, range, rhythm, consonance and dissonance, to get your ideas across.

- Use space (rests) to frame your musical statements; they will be more effective.

- Learn some double-time (sixteenth note) licks that appeal to you; use them when you need more density, motion, or rhythmic excitement.

- Listen to the band. You are not improvising in a vacuum. Trade ideas back and forth.

- Listen to and watch the audience, and feel the mood of the overall environment.

- Constantly try to play beyond your own technical and conceptual limitations.

2. "Outside" playing *(example: CD track 27)*

If we are looking for note choices that seem unpredictable, "modern," or maybe even harsh, we must look outside of the key that is serving as our tonal environment. This may involve setting up a second tonal center, or simply avoiding the "inside" notes.

This is not always easy to achieve. First, you don't want your outside ideas to sound like a mistake. On the other hand, to a modern listener, nearly anything can sound like a tension note. Consider the following example, sounding a D triad over a Cmaj7 chord; this could come across as a single tonality, Cmaj9 (♯11, 13).

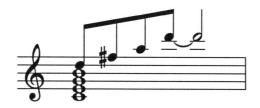

Here are a few points regarding outside playing:

- Try pretending that you are in a different key. The more conflicting accidentals there are in the key you are overlaying, the harsher the effect. Thus, overlaying G major on a C major tonality is mild; C♯ major over C major has much more bite.

- You must play assertively to make your "outside" placement obvious.

- Playing sequences is a good way to draw the listener into an overlaid tonality. First play a lick inside, then repeat the same shape in a different key. Pentatonic motives are often used in this way.

- Outside playing is easier, and perhaps more effective, in tunes with chords that don't change too quickly.

- "Polytonal" and "upper structure" are overlapping concepts. "Outside" is a related idea, but very much a matter of personal judgement.

3. About "originality"

Western music over the last five centuries has valued "progress"; each generation seems to build on the achievements of the last. We have come to believe that it is the artist's duty not just to entertain, but also to push the boundaries of expression. We especially respect the example of artists like Mozart, Beethoven, Debussy, Parker, Miles, and Coltrane—or Monet, Van Gogh, and Picasso—who mastered their craft and then created new modes of expression.

In the last century, change has come increasingly quickly. In both jazz and classical music, artists have sought to achieve "originality" by discarding existing concepts of melody and harmony. This has brought us to "cutting edge" artists like John Cage, who treated all sound as music, including random sound. And that was fifty years ago! Outside playing, at this point in time, is an old idea.

It can be argued that achieving novelty simply by breaking rules is an idea that may be played out. Progress will come by itself, in a more natural way, and in the meantime, we have all the resources of the world's cultures, as well as unfinished business of the last 1000 years of Western culture, to work with.

These are issues worth thinking about. You can come to your own conclusions about how to balance tradition and newness, craftsmanship and originality, entertainment and spirituality, in your own work.

4. Exercises

- Find another musician to comp for you—have him or her repeat a single chord, in rhythm, on piano or guitar. Try playing against this background, in different keys. Try a half step up, a half step down, a major second up or down, and so forth. Listen carefully to the sound of each superimposed tonality. (If you don't have another musician to help you, make your own accompaniment tape.)

- Try some "free" playing, unaccompanied. This means improvising without following harmonies, key centers, or time signatures. In fact, try *not* to follow any of those constraints. Your organizing principles should be emotion and expression. Keep playing for as long as possible.

- Try the same thing with a group of other musicians, any instrumentation, whoever is interested. Keep playing for as long as possible.

Chapter 8

Learning Tunes

To play mainstream jazz, you need to know the repertoire. There are hundreds of standards; you should make an effort to know as many as possible. Start with the tunes mentioned in this book—most of them are on the "must know" list.

A basic familiarity with a tune will enable you to "fake" your way through a solo ("fake" is not a negative term—it means to rely on your ear). On another level, you can learn the melody and progression in detail. The better you understand a tune, the more your imagination has to work with.

1. Suggestions for learning tunes

First, learn the melody. When improvising, you should always have the melody in the back of your mind. If the tune was originally conceived with lyrics, learn them. You will phrase the melody effectively, and better understand the feeling that the composer intended to convey (e.g., "Night and Day," or "April in Paris"). Note: Most bop standards were written as instrumentals (e.g., "Donna Lee," or "Blue Monk"). Words added later to these tunes by vocalists are usually not especially pertinent to understanding the piece.

Analyze the tune's chord progression. Look for key centers, and look for "harmonic clichés" (see Chapter 3) that drive the chord progression.

Check the *guide tones*. The notes driving harmonic movement are usually the third and seventh of the chords. If you trace these notes through a tune, you will see that they generally form two *guide tone lines* (we have seen this concept in blues and in Rhythm changes). Pay special attention to the thirds (leading tones) of all dominants and secondary dominants. Other strong notes are the ♭6 of the key for subdominant minor chords, and new accidentals as they appear in the progression.

Make sure that you know exactly how each chord is constructed, and learn the scales that fit each chord.

2. Tips on analyzing harmony

- Chords usually function in one of three ways: *tonic* (at rest), *dominant* (tension), or *dominant preparation* (neutral). The II V I progression is a perfect example: II is dominant preparation, V is dominant, I is tonic. A *tonic substitute* (III or VI, for example) may provide a partial resolution after a V; a *dominant substitute* (♭IIdom or ♭VIIdom, for example) may provide tension without actually being a V.

- If you see a minor 7 chord followed by a dominant 7, suspect II V in a major key. If you see a minor 7♭5 followed by dominant ♭9, suspect II V in a minor key.

- If you can't explain a chord in the key you are in, then look ahead to where the progression may be going.

- When analyzing a progression, you will usually find the following to be true:

  Major 7 chords will be I or IV in a major key, possibly ♭VI in minor.

  Dominant 7 chords will be V, but in a blues may be I or IV; could also be secondary dominant, ♭VIIdom, ♭IIdom (sub V), or ♭VI in minor.

  Augmented 7 chords (dominant ♯5) will be V.

  Dominant chords with major 9 or ♯11 imply V in major, V of II, sub V, or ♭VIIdom; extensions ♭9, ♯9, or ♭13 (or "alt") imply V in minor, or a secondary dominant headed for a minor chord.

  Minor 7 chords will be II, III, or VI in major, I or IV in minor, or I in dorian.

  Minor 7♭5 chords will be II in minor (sometimes this chord acts as a pivot, introduced as VII or ♯IV in major, then treated as II in minor).

  Diminished 7 chords will be either *passing* chords, providing stepwise passing notes connecting two other chords, or else will function like dominant ♭9 with the root omitted (*incomplete dominant ♭9*, see Chapter 4, part 5).

  Minor 6 or minor ♯7 chords will be I or IV in minor. Sometimes minor 6 chords are misnamed minor 7♭5 chords (see part 4 of this chapter).

3. Form

You must understand the form of each tune. Standard tunes usually follow one of several typical forms; we have already studied two of the most common: 12-bar blues, and 32-bar AABA (as seen in Rhythm changes).

In describing form, we use capital letters for melodic units. Usually these units will be 8 measures long, although sometimes a letter will represent a 4- or 16-bar unit, or some less common variation. Sections showing only slight differences are often represented as A^1, A^2, etc.

Note: Sometimes there is more than one "right" way to depict a form.

Here are a few other common forms, and tunes that use them:

>AABC ("Autumn Leaves," "Forest Flower")
>
>ABAC ("Out of Nowhere," "It Had to be You")
>
>AAB ("Song for my Father," "Once I Loved")
>
>$ABAB^1$ ("Shiny Stockings," "Just Friends")
>
>AA^1BA^2 ("All the Things You Are")

Musicians often refer to the B section of an AABA or AAB tune as the *bridge*. Bridges usually involve a temporary change of key.

Many standards were originally written with a lead-in section called a *verse*. Most verses are not used today by jazz instrumentalists; vocalists sometimes include them. For just a few tunes, the verse has remained an integral part of the piece (e.g., Billy Strayhorn's "Lush Life," Hoagy Carmichael's "Stardust").

In traditional songwriter's parlance, the A section following the verse is sometimes called the *chorus* or *refrain*; the B section (bridge) is sometimes called the *release* or *channel*. Jazz musicians generally use the word "chorus" differently, to mean "one time through the solo form," as in, "take as many choruses as you like."

4. Interpreting lead sheets

The standard printed format for jazz improvisers is the *lead sheet*, showing only the basic melody and chord symbols. These are often found in collections called *fake books*. When you are working from a lead sheet, keep these important points in mind:

- Do not take correctness for granted. You will often encounter mistakes in melody or chords, or interpretations that can be improved upon. Examine lead sheets critically; compare different sources for the same song, and/or check against recorded versions.

- Melodies are usually printed in their simplest form. Performers must supply their own interpretation. It will sound silly to play as written, if a melody is shown in quarter notes and half notes.

- Chords, too, are often shown in simplest form (usually as seventh chords), with performers free to interpret. Extensions—ninths, elevenths, thirteenths—are left to your discretion. If a pianist sees "Cmaj7" on a lead sheet, he or she might play C6, Cmaj9, Cmaj7($\sharp$5), Cmaj7($\sharp$11), a C triad, or C6/9, depending on harmonic context and personal taste. Soloists can do the same thing.

- Chords are sometimes misnamed. For example, Cm6 might appear where Am7$\flat$5 would make more sense (same notes, but A is the functional root).

- Many older lead sheets show superfluous chord changes. This is usually done in an effort to convey a specific arrangement by using symbols. Observing these chords can work, if you can figure out what the lead sheet's author had in mind. More often, you will want to delete unnecessary changes.

- Some fake books (e.g., the *New Real Book*) show melody notes as part of the chord. For example, if the melody is on the note A, played over a C7 chord, the chord might appear as "C13." In cases like this, you are probably better off thinking of the chord simply as C7, open to further interpretation. Playing the chord as C13 every time would be needlessly restrictive.

5. Memorizing tunes

Begin memorizing tunes, melody and changes. You will improvise with more meaning and directness when you are not reading. You will hear your fellow musicians better, and you will phrase more effectively.

Tunes may be grouped by their harmonic structure; this will help you in understanding and memorizing the changes.

Many jazz tunes (especially bop-era) are original melodies written over chord progressions similar to those of pre-existing standards. The two most basic groups are blues tunes, and tunes built on Rhythm changes. Rhythm tunes include "Anthropology," "Cottontail," "Dexterity," "Flintstones" theme, "Moose the Mooche," "Lester Leaps In," "Oleo," "Shaw 'Nuff," "Steeplechase," "The Theme," "Who's Got Rhythm," and many more.

Here are some other tunes with chords similar to earlier standards:

- Benny Harris and Charlie Parker's "Ornithology" ("How High the Moon").

- Parker's "Scrapple from the Apple" ("Honeysuckle Rose" A section, "Rhythm" bridge), "Quasimodo" ("Embraceable You"), and "Donna Lee" ("Indiana").

- Jackie McLean's "Dig" ("Sweet Georgia Brown").

- Miles Davis' "Half Nelson" ("Lady Bird").

- Tadd Dameron's "Hot House" ("What is This Thing Called Love").

- Dizzy Gillespie's "Groovin' High" ("Whispering").

- Thelonious Monk's "Hackensack" ("Lady Be Good").

- Dexter Gordon's "Fried Bananas" ("It Could Happen to You").

- Duke Ellington's "In a Mellotone" ("Rose Room").

The overlaid bop melodies often provide instructive examples of how to solo over those changes.

Memorizing changes becomes easier if you can reduce a progression to harmonic clichés. The list below shows groups of tunes with harmonic similarities.

Most of these tunes are readily available in fake books. You should take the time to study these tunes and compare their progressions (think Roman numerals). You will be rewarded with interesting and educational insights.

- "Out of Nowhere," "Bye Bye Blues," "Triste," "Look to the Sky," "Meditation," "Dreamer," theme to original "Star Trek" TV show (compare overall structure).

- "There Will Never Be Another You," "Weaver of Dreams," "The Masquerade is Over," "Bluesette," "Blues for Alice," "Confirmation," "Lover Come Back to Me."

- "Do Nothing 'til You Hear From Me," "Cherokee," "The Nearness of You," "Batida Diferente," "Misty."

- "Take the 'A' Train," "Jersey Bounce," "Watch What Happens," "Girl from Ipanema," "Exactly Like You," "So Danço Samba," "Desafinado" (compare A sections).

- "On the Sunny Side of the Street," "Georgia On My Mind," "Five Foot Two," "All of Me," "Charleston," "Basin Street Blues," "That's Life," "You're Nobody 'til Somebody Loves You," "Clarinet Marmalade" (first chord change, I to IIIdom).

- "Angel Eyes," "This Masquerade," "Everything Happens to Me," "Do You Know What it Means to Miss New Orleans" (B sections).

- "Yardbird Suite," "I've Got My Love to Keep Me Warm" (B sections).

- "A Night in Tunisia," "Alone Together" (both have minor A sections; similar B sections).

- "Polka Dots and Moonbeams," "A Nightingale Sang in Berkeley Square," "Desafinado" (bridges in the region of the III).

- "Groovin' High," "Dream," "Summer Samba," "My Little Boat," "I Remember You" (first change, I to a II V beginning on the ♯4 of the key).

- "Airegin," "Tickle Toe."

- "Tangerine," "I Love You," "I Hadn't Anyone 'Til You," "If I Were a Bell," "Triste," "I'm Old Fashioned" (brief change of key, moving up a major third).

- "Autumn Leaves," "Beautiful Love," "Black Orpheus," "Lullaby of Birdland," "My Shining Hour" (modulation between relative major and relative minor).

- "Satin Doll," "So Danço Samba" (bridge sections).

- "Don't Get Around Much Anymore," "Stormy Weather," "Gee Baby, Ain't I Good to You" (bridge sections).

- "Laura," "Tune Up," "Solar," "No Me Esqueca," "The End of a Love Affair," "Star Eyes," "Joy Spring" (bridge), "One Note Samba" (bridge) (II V moving down in whole steps).

- "Ceora," "Shiny Stockings" (bars 9-16 of both tunes); "Satin Doll" (II V moving up in whole steps).

- "Invitation," "Cherokee," "One Note Samba" (when these tunes are played in their usual keys, each B section begins with II V in D♭ major, followed by II V moving down in whole steps).

- "Stardust," "After You've Gone," "Moonglow," "Just Friends" (beginning: IV to IVm).

- "One Note Samba," Rhythm changes (A sections).

- "In Walked Bud," "Blue Skies" (A sections).

- Blues, "Wave" (A section).

6. Exercises

Pick one tune from the above list. Learn the melody. Next, analyze the progression. Compare the other tunes in the same group. Then work on the following exercises.

- Embellish the melody. At first stick fairly close to the melody, then play variations that increasingly diverge from the melody.

- Arpeggiate each chord in the tune.

- Play each chord scale. Remember that there may be more than one possible scale for a given chord, especially for dominants.

- Play patterns or licks over each chord. Base licks on the tonic of each chord.

- Pick a one- or two-bar melodic shape (motive), and repeat it over the progression with only a little variation, changing accidentals as required by the key centers. Try to include guide tones and other strong notes.

- Play a continuous line with a particular constant shape or melodic curve over the tune's changes, using chord tones and chord scales.

- Play as above, but this time let your own sense of continuity determine the melodic curve.

- Improvise three choruses, working with "density." Begin sparsely, with many rests, building until the last chorus, which should be very dense with notes.

- Play as above, but this time build with emotion instead of density: first chorus relaxed, quiet; second chorus "normal"; third chorus intense, loud. Or try three choruses with a string of different emotions (bored, passionate, aggressive, etc.).

- Take any of the above approaches, but stretch over as many choruses as you can maintain.

- Listen to recorded versions of the tune by different jazz artists.

- Transcribe solos from recordings. This a time-honored way to learn the vocabulary of jazz, and improve your hearing. You can put the solo on paper, or just copy it on your instrument. You can also play and analyze published transcriptions, although you will miss the benefit of doing the work yourself.

- Compose (write down) a solo that seems effective to you.

- Improvise mentally.

Chapter 9

Sample Analysis: "After You've Gone"

In this chapter, we will explore one tune in detail, with special attention to improvising approaches. When you understand the method presented here, you will be able to apply it to other tunes.

Play through and analyze the sample solo in part 5 for an illustration of how theory concepts can be used (or ignored!) in an actual playing situation.

This chapter will be most meaningful to you if you can rehearse the tune with a group. If you don't have this opportunity, use the play-along track *(CD track 30)*. Chord charts are in Appendix C.

1. Lead sheet and analysis *(example: CD track 28)*

On the next page is a lead sheet for Henry Creamer and Turner Layton's "After You've Gone," with a chordal analysis written above each line. Play through the tune, preferably on piano (chords in left hand, melody in right). If your keyboard skills are not up to this, then run through the melody on your instrument, using the CD play-along track.

The lead sheet shows the melody in its most basic form; feel free to interpret it as you see fit (as in the rendition on the CD).

The form of the tune is ABAC, with the A and B sections eight measures each. The C section is 16 measures. Altogether this adds up to 40 measures, a non-standard length.

The tune was originally written with a verse, or lead-in. It has been omitted here; jazz musicians today do not use it.

After You've Gone

Creamer/Layton

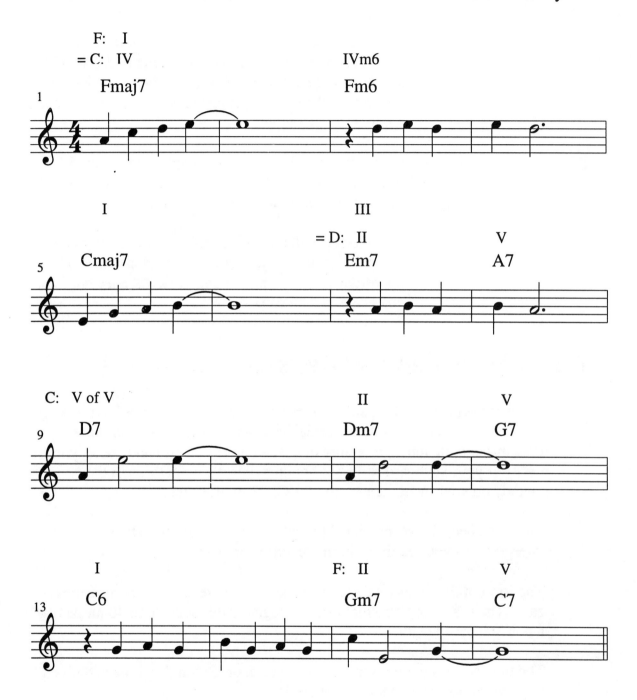

2. About this tune

"After You've Gone" was originally written in eighth-note rhythm, as shown below, to be played at a moderate or slow tempo, as a ballad.

Today, this tune is usually played up-tempo, with a "double time feel." This means that as compared to the original, the beat is doubled up by the rhythm section. This is not really "double time," since the speed of the progression does not double—notice that each measure of the original is turned into two measures in our lead sheet. The tune has been re-notated here to reflect this feel, and is played this way on the CD.

The tune is often played with a four bar "stop-time" break in bars 13-16, and again in bars 37-40. The soloist should continue through the breaks, with the rhythm section tacet. If another player is about to solo on the next chorus, he or she would start over the break in bars 37-40, as a pickup into the new solo.

A drummer friend of mine, who began performing in 1926, recalls that at that time the tune was usually played with an arrangement that began with one chorus of the slow version, then broke into the more energetic double time feel. The breaks were a standard feature then, too.

The original sheet music was for voice with piano accompaniment, and did not show chord symbols. In setting up our lead sheet, I have mostly kept the original harmonies, but have made a few adjustments.

The piano part incorporated some nice voice leading in the bass. I have opted to leave these notes off, rather than try to indicate them with slashes (e.g., "Cmaj7/E"). I have done this in the interests of simplification, and because a modern bass player does not need to observe the restrictions of the original arrangement. I have also changed some dominant chords to II V sequences to reflect contemporary harmonic concepts.

The original piano part included a short counter-line in bars 16-17 and 40-1 (setting up the repeat) which has become part of the tune as it is usually played. The line may be played by soloist or accompanist, or it may only be implied:

 etc.

"After You've Gone" has been recorded by many jazz artists and popular vocalists. A partial list includes Louis Armstrong, Count Basie, Sidney Bechet, Nat Cole, Bing Crosby, Eddie "Lockjaw" Davis, Tommy Dorsey, Roy Eldridge, Clare Fischer, Judy Garland, Benny Goodman, Stephane Grappelli, Lionel Hampton, Shirley Horn, Wynton Marsalis, Frank Morgan, Charlie Parker, Django Reinhardt, Zoot Sims, Frank Sinatra, Bessie Smith, Sonny Stitt, Art Tatum, Cal Tjader, Sarah Vaughan, Fats Waller, Teddy Wilson, and Lester Young.

This tune was first published in 1918, and is in the public domain.

3. Lyrics

Below are the lyrics. When this tune is played up-tempo, the tone is a lot less sentimental.

After you've gone, and left me crying
After you've gone, there's no denying
You'll feel blue, you'll feel sad
You'll miss the dearest pal you've ever had

There'll come a time, now don't forget it
There'll come a time, when you'll regret it
Some day, when you grow lonely
Your heart will break like mine and you'll want me only

After you've gone, after you've gone away.

4. Bar-by-bar comments

Measure	Chord	Comments

1-2   Fmaj7   Overall, the tune is in the key of C major, and this is a IV chord. Therefore, you could improvise using an F lydian scale. However, in a "local" sense, we could be in F major here, and an F major scale sounds fine.

You should be aware of the guide tone line that includes the note A in this chord, moving to A♭ in measures 3-4, to G in measure 5.

This chord could be played as F6, F6/9, Fmaj9, or Fmaj7(♯11); these are interchangeable. Although each of these chords sounds a little different, they all function the same way. You could try an upper structure II over an Fmaj7 here.

3-4   Fm6   This is the "subdominant minor" harmonic cliché. The appropriate scale would be F melodic minor. Also possible: C natural minor or F dorian.

Be aware of the note A♭, and its place in the guide tone line.

Interchangeable chords here would be Fm♯7 (use F melodic minor), or B♭7 (use B♭ lydian dominant). Or you could play Fm6 to B♭7, one bar each. Note that the corresponding scales, F melodic minor and B♭ lydian dominant, are actually the *same scale*, with different roots (the two scales are modes of each other).

Measure	Chord	Comments
5-6	Cmaj7	Tonic chord; use a C major scale. Some players might use C lydian. The original piano part showed an E in the bass. If you voice the chord without a root, and use the E bass note, you are really playing Em7, a perfectly reasonable substitution. If you use Em7 here, the scale could be E phrygian, implying the key of C major. However, this would make the ninth of the chord F♮, or ♭9, not a great choice for a minor 7 chord voicing. F♯ would sound better, if you must have a 9. In that case, the scale becomes E dorian. Interchangeable chords: C6, C6/9, Cmaj9, maybe Cmaj7(♯11).
7	Em7	The original sheet music showed bars 7-8 as two bars of A7. Here we are treating these bars as a II V in D, a standard way to make a plain dominant chord more improv-friendly. Use E dorian.
8	A7	This dominant chord is setting up the D7 in the next bar. You could look at it as a V in the key of D, or as a V of II in the key of C. Generally, a V of II implies a ♭9. Here, however, the melody includes a B♮, so the chord would also take a major 9 when backing up the melody. The scale for the A9 is A mixolydian. But during solos, when the melody is not a consideration, any sort of dominant chord or scale is possible. Try A7♭9 (corresponding scale is B♭ diminished), or A7alt (A altered scale). Over either of these chords, you could also try D harmonic minor, or a D blues scale. Each of these choices will lead you to different ideas for licks. Some notes may clash a bit with the chord, so use your ear.

Measure	Chord	Comments
		For solos, the sub V chord, E♭7, works here. The corresponding scale is lydian dominant; the upper structure is II (F triad).
		Be especially aware of the note C♯, a "new note" in the progression, and the note that drives the chord (the leading tone, aimed at the D in the next measure)
9-10	D7	Again, the melody note (A) suggests a less chromatic sound. The scale choice here would be D mixolydian.
		The melody is not a problem during solos; try D lydian dominant (this usually is a good scale for a V of V). The corresponding upper structure is II (E major triad).
		Be aware of the note F♯, the third of this secondary dominant, a "new note," a leading tone, and the note that drives the progression.
11	Dm7	Although the original music showed two bars of G7 here, we will use a standard II V cadence. The corresponding scale is dorian.
12	G7	V in C major. The melody note is on the perfect fifth, which once again prevents altering the chord much when backing up the melody. This outlook would suggest using a G7 (9, 13); the corresponding scale is mixolydian. G7♭9 could work here (use G♯ diminished scale).
		Another possibility would be to use a G7 with extensions 9 and 13 for two beats, then move to a G7alt or G7♭9, creating some chromatic voice leading.

Measure	Chord	Comments
		In soloing or comping for solos, there is no reason to limit the tensions here. Try G7+ (use G whole tone scale), G7alt (use G altered scale) or G7♭9 (use G♯ diminished scale).
		Upper structures for G7alt could be ♭II minor (A♭ minor triad), ♭VI (E♭ triad). or ♯IVdom (C♯7—like subV). For G7♭9, upper structure VI (E triad).
		For solos, try a C blues scale here. This trick is almost always good: Over a V, use the blues scale of the tonic chord which is to follow.
13-14	C6	Tonic chord; use a C major scale. This is where the stop-time occurs. The rhythm section will hit beat one, then drop out for three or four bars while the soloist continues with melody or improvisation. For this one beat, it is probably best not to use a substitution with a different root, since we want the sound of a resolution. You can still use C6, Cmaj7, C6/9, and Cmaj9 interchangeably. For a little funkyness, try playing this chord as C7♯9.
		For the soloist, anything goes, since there is no accompaniment to worry about. Play with a C major or a C blues scale for an inside sound. For a more outside approach, play up a half step for three measures, then go back to a C7 sound in measure 16. Or you could interpolate an entire substitute chord progression in the break, while the rhythm section is tacet.
		How about "Coltrane changes" here? Bars 13-16 could be Cmaj7 E♭7 A♭maj7 B7 Emaj7 G7 Gm7 C7, two beats each (see John Coltrane's "Giant Steps" or "Countdown"). Of course, this would probably be inappropriate for a dixieland or swing gig.

Measure	Chord	Comments
15	Gm7	The original music showed two bars of C7, setting up the return to Fmaj7 in the second A section. We have turned this into a II V, as in bars 5-6 and 11-12. Use G dorian; the "new" note B♭ is the strong note here. If you are playing this tune with the traditional break in bar 13, the rhythm section might choose to remain tacet in bars 15 and/or 16.
16	C7	V in F. The melody note, G, once again suggests a non-chromatic version of C7. As in measures 7-8, one way around this is to play two beats of C9 or C13, followed by two beats of C7♭9 or C7alt. In soloing and in comping for solos, there is no problem with playing tensions on this chord. Soloists will almost certainly want to play all sorts of alterations here, to set up the resolution to Fmaj7 in the next measure.
17-24		The first 8 measures of the second A section are exactly like the first 8 measures of the tune.
25	Dm6	Instead of resolving to D7, as in bar 9, this time the A7 resolves into a new temporary key center, D minor. Tonic minor chords are often played as minor 6 or minor ♯7 (use D melodic minor), although Dm7 is possible here too (dorian or natural minor). Bars 25-27 are all in the key of D minor, opening up the possibility of simply improvising over all three bars with a D minor scale. However, minor has several forms, so the question arises, "what kind of minor?" Natural minor, harmonic minor, melodic minor, and dorian all have the same notes from root to fifth; these scales only differ in their sixth and seventh scale steps. You can use "D minor" here if you note how these two scale steps relate to the chords. The D blues scale, or D minor pentatonic, can also work anywhere in bars 25-27.

Measure	Chord	Comments

This may be a good place to remind you that all of our scale suggestions are merely guidelines for finding a set of consonant notes to fit a chord. Actually, *any note can work over any chord*, if it is used right. For example, The note E♭ does not seem to fit over the Dm6. But it could be used to good effect—as a passing tone, as a chromatic approach to a chord tone, or as an intentional dissonance. Follow your ear!

26   Em7♭5   II in D minor; use E locrian or E locrian ♯2. If you prefer to think in D minor, use D natural minor or D harmonic minor.

Using E locrian ♯2 allows a major 9 (F♯) on this chord. If you are thinking in either E locrian or D natural minor, the naturally-occurring 9 would be a ♭9 (F♮), not a good sound for voicing this chord. The locrian ♯2 idea sets up a nice chromatic line moving from F♯ here, to F♮ in the next bar (use A7alt), to E in bar 28. This will work better for solos than in backing up the melody.

A7♭9   For the head, it is probably better to play this chord as A7♭9 with a major 13, implying a B♭ diminished scale, and an upper structure VI (F♯ triad). For solos, another possibility is A7alt, with an A altered scale.

The difference between these scales is that the diminished scale includes a perfect fifth and a major 13, while the altered scale includes a ♭13 in their place. Both scales include 1, ♭9, ♯9, 3, ♯11, and ♭7.

If you are thinking in D minor, the scale to use here could be D natural minor or D harmonic minor.

Measure	Chord	Comments
27	Dm6	See comments for measure 25.
28	Fm6	See comments for measure 3. The guide tone line here would run from the A in the previous chord, to the A♭ here, to the G in the Cmaj7 that follows.
29	Cmaj7	Tonic chord; use C major scale. Interchangeable chords are C6, C6/9, Cmaj9.
30	E7	V of VI. Be aware of the leading tone, G♯. The original bass line, by the way, used a G in bar 29, to G♯ here, to A in the next bar.
		The melody in this bar does not cause a problem with alterations. The note B on beat 4 is unaccented, and won't clash too much with an altered fifth. Just about any version of E7 will work. For soloing or comping for solos, try substituting B♭7 (use B♭ lydian dominant).
31	Am7	The mode that fits VI in major is aeolian (natural minor). Dorian works here as well. Melodic or harmonic minor are possible, but have a little more bite.
32	E♭dim7	As you may recall, diminished chords can function either as passing chords or as "incomplete dominants." This is a passing chord, taking us back to the tonic. Use an E♭ diminished scale.
		The original harmony here was D7. It worked fairly well because of the voice leading in the piano part, but to my ear the diminished chord is better. Of course, you could also use F♯dim7, Adim7, or Cdim7, since they are exactly the same as E♭dim7, with a different specified bass note.
		B7 or B7♭9 is possible here. It is related to E♭dim7 and to D7 via the diminished scale that all three chords share.

Measure	Chord	Comments
33	C6	See comments for measure 29. Note that bars 33-36 are a basic turnaround. For solos, you might try some other standard turnarounds (see Chapter 3, part 11).
34	A7	V of II; be aware of the note C♯. Since the melody is on the perfect fifth, don't alter the fifth on beat one when backing up the melody. As in bar 12, you could play with major 9 and 13 for two beats, then with ♭9 and/or ♭13 for two beats, to get some chromatic color. For solos, any extensions will work.
35	Dm7	See measure 11.
36	G7	The melody is on the perfect fifth and major sixth. When backing up the melody, do not use G7alt, although G7♭9(13) is good here. The corresponding scale is G♯ diminished. For solo choruses, any sort of dominant chord is possible; see comments for measure 12.
37-38	Cmaj7	See comments for measures 13-14.
39-40	Gm7 C7	See comments for measures 15-16.

5. Sample solo *(example: CD track 29; play-along: CD track 30)*

Following is a sample solo for "After You've Gone." Play through it, comparing it to the bar-by-bar analysis. Note that musical ideas are expressed as licks and phrases—chords and scales are only background concepts. If a lick sounds good to you, lift it and practice it in 12 keys. You will find this solo transcribed for B♭ and E♭ instruments in Appendix C. The solo begins with the four-bar pickup in bar 37, at the end of the head.

You can practice soloing with the play-along track (four choruses). For a chart, use the lead sheet in part 1. If you play a transposing instrument, you could rewrite the lead sheet in your key, or better yet, transpose the melody and chords in your head. Chord charts can be found in Appendix C.

(begin next solo)

6. Exercises

- Make sure that you completely understand the bar-by-bar analysis.

- Compare the solo to the analysis. Note areas where scales or upper structures are used, and areas where they are not.

- Note other factors that contribute to determining the solo's shape: motivic development, melodic curve, phrasing, range, rhythmic activity.

- Learn "After You've Gone," using the suggestions in Chapter 8. Practice soloing on the changes unaccompanied, with the play-along, or with other musicians.

- Write a set of solo changes for "After You've Gone" using substitutions. Don't worry about making the chords fit the melody. Practice soloing on your progression.

- Write a new head for your new progression.

- Do a bar-by-bar analysis for one other tune that you wish to make part of your repertoire.

Chapter 10

Suggestions for Further Study

Each individual follows his or her unique approach to learning jazz. One person may relate better to a theory-oriented approach, while another with a great ear may go far with little theory knowledge. There is more than one right way to learn.

In this chapter we will discuss some universally accepted ways to develop skills as a jazz improviser. You can make your own decisions about which approaches will benefit you the most.

1. Listen, practice, analyze, perform

Virtually all musicians would agree that these four elements are essential to becoming a good jazz player:

Listen.

Extensive listening is important—both casual and analytical.

This is the only way to absorb and understand the jazz language. Check out the recorded performances of the masters, on all instruments, not just your own. Attend live jazz performances as often as you can—improvised music is most relevent in the time and place that it is created. Listen critically and appreciatively to your fellow players, when you are rehearsing.

Keep your ears open to all types of music. You can find inspiration, perspective, and learning opportunities in everything from classical music, to the music of other cultures, to supermarket background music.

Practice.

Practicing is the time that we devote to eliminating weak spots in our technique, expanding our capabilities, and becoming increasingly familiar with our instrument.

Since time immemorial, musicians have practiced scales and arpeggios, since music often follows these shapes. Extending this idea to other basic shapes (e.g., scales in broken thirds, or II V I patterns), we can prepare ourselves to express any musical idea that occurs to us.

You need to do more than just go through the motions of playing your exercises. Keep your attention on your work. When you detect a weak spot in your playing, invent an exercise to address the problem, and work through it.

Suggestions for practice routines are covered in parts 2 and 3 of this chapter.

Analyze.

Analyze tunes and transcribe solos, to see how theory relates to actual music. Transcribing is a time-honored way to learn the jazz vocabulary—you can simultaneously learn licks, develop your hearing, and internalize the musical thought process of the artist you are studying. You could transcribe on paper, or just copy the sounds on your instrument. You could learn entire solos, or just fragments.

There are many other excellent jazz theory books available. Every writer has a somewhat different outlook; you can learn from all of them, and eventually will develop your own perspective. See Appendix D for some recommended follow-ups for this book.

Perform.

Music is all about communication. Playing for other people is really where the most direct learning takes place.

If you don't have a band to play with, find one or form one!

2. Practice routines

Your available practice time should be used as efficiently as possible.

You should allocate your time as you see fit, among the following (these categories may overlap):

- Urgent needs and projects (such as parts for tomorrow's concert).

- Exercises for basic technique, that will benefit you in the long term (such as scales and arpeggios).

- Licks and phrases that you wish to add to your working vocabulary for improvising (e.g., licks from transcribed solos, or II V I patterns).

- Reading—working on written pieces, or improving your sightreading.

- Improvising—that is, practicing the use of your creative process.

- Learning tunes.

- Instrument-specific exercises (like long tones or overtones on saxophone).

- Reviewing items of study that you have previously covered, to keep them current.

In the chapter-end exercises, and in Chapter 8, you have already encountered some of these approaches. The next part of this chapter lists some "basic technique" exercises, valid for all instruments, that virtually all musicians have found useful.

3. Exercises for basic technique *(examples: CD track 31)*

Your goal, impossible to fully achieve, is to be in total control of all scales and chords, and all the shapes that derive from them, so that you are ready to play anything, in any key, at any tempo.

Start with the basics: one-octave scales and root-position chords, in all keys. As you master each basic shape, add more complex variations to your practice routine. The exercises below will get you started; you can devise your own extensions.

Play all of these exercises both with a straight beat and with a swing beat. Begin each exercise by playing as slowly as necessary to achieve smoothness and accuracy; then gradually increase the tempo with each repetition, until you are playing by reaction, rather than intellectualizing.

- Play all 12 major scales, one octave. Move clockwise along the circle of fifths. First learn separately, then connect scales.

To develop versatility in thinking and technique, you should play each exercise with variations, as in the examples below.

- Extend scales to top and bottom of instrumental range.

- Play each mode, as above.

- Apply the above approach to arpeggios: first triads, then seventh chords. Learn each arpeggio separately, then try the following pattern, with the third of each chord moving to the root of the next chord along the circle:

 etc.

- Move scales and arpeggios up chromatically, covering range of instrument from low to high; then move chromatically down.

 etc.

- 1 2 3 5 in all keys; move along circle or chromatically (also 5 3 2 1, 1 2 ♭3 5, and 5 ♭3 2 1).

 etc.

- Major scales with a ♭7 added ("bebop dominant"); move along circle or chromatically.

 etc.

etc.

- Major scales and other modes in diatonic thirds; do this in every key. Also try fourths, fifths, etc.

- Major-key triads on each scale tone; seventh chords on each scale tone. Play in every key, moving along circle or chromatically.

- Practice licks and II V patterns, in all keys, moving along circle or chromatically. Think numbers as you play. Try blues licks, as well as scale-based licks. Practice ideas that appeal to you, either composed by yourself, or from recorded solos. Try extracting some licks from the sample solos in this book. For a few suggested II V ideas, see Appendix A.

- To challenge yourself further, try moving licks, chords, and scales up and down by whole step, by minor third, by major third, or by diminished fifth:

 etc.

- As you master each exercise, turn it into a more complex one. For example, create a double-time lick (sixteenth notes) by doubling the tempo of a pattern that you have already learned in eighth notes. Or combine two eighth-note licks to make one longer lick:

At this point, after looking over and playing these "basic technique" exercises, you can understand the principle behind them: Begin with basic shapes, and gradually alter them, or move them in different ways, to expand the scope of your ability. You should now be able to adapt this approach to your own level and your own needs.

A few general suggestions:

Sing each exercise; it helps internalize the sound.

A metronome is useful.

Try playing each exercise mentally. Imagine the fingerings and sound. You can do this on the bus, at the dentist's office, or while trying to get to sleep at night.

Classical method books (e.g., Arban, Klosé, Hanon, deVille) are full of this sort of exercise. Try some of their patterns, but play in every key, and don't use the sheet music.

Appendix A

II V I licks *(examples: CD track 32)*

Because II V I is a fundamental harmonic unit, you need to understand it thoroughly. Learning licks to fit this sequence is a practical and time-honored way to internalize its sound. *The object is not just to have patterns ready to plug into a solo, but more importantly, to improve your ability to hear the progression.*

The patterns below are shown in C; you should practice them in all 12 keys.

- This one-bar II V pattern is a good one to start with. It consists of a root position arpeggio of the II chord, with the seventh resolving to the third, then the root, of the V chord:

- If we delay the pattern by two beats, it becomes a two-bar lick:

- Here is a rhythmic variation:

- Next, reverse the direction of the II chord, running it down from the seventh:

- Here is the two-bar version:

- Next, add a few notes to include the I chord:

- This pattern runs the II chord from third to ninth:

- Here is a scale-oriented II V I lick:

- Here is a lick with both scalar and chordal elements:

- You can find quite a few II V I licks in the repertoire of classical and jazz standards. Here is one from Alexander Borodin's "Prince Igor" (also known as the pop tune "Stranger in Paradise"):

Also check out the beginning of David Raksin's "Laura," (II V I over 4 bars), and Fats Waller's "Honeysuckle Rose" (II V in one bar). These are favorite bop quotes.

- Below are a few more licks to try. You may notice that in many patterns, the notes played over the V include chromatic tension notes. These color tones make the sound of the V more interesting, and enhance the inherent tension of the V chord.

- Finally, here are a few patterns for II V I in minor:

- For more licks, see other jazz theory books or improvisation methods. Better yet, compose or transcribe a few of your own.

Appendix B

The logic behind the chord scale system

The chord scale system presented in this book is generally accepted in the jazz world today. Nearly all improvisation method books use it, and most jazz musicians educated since the 1970s are aware of it. There is a good reason why this group of scales has proved to be so useful: A scale for every chord can be found in the set of 16 scale types that includes *seven modes of major, seven modes of melodic minor, the diminished scale,* and *the whole tone scale.*

These 16 scale types include every way that an octave can be filled in a linear way, with whole steps and half steps. Mathematically, there are no additional possibilities; the explanation is given below.

Our system assumes that seventh chords are the basic chordal unit. To find a corresponding scale, we fill in the spaces between chord tones with tension notes that generally (but not always) lie a whole step above each chord tone.

Any scale filling an octave must have an even number of half steps. There are exactly 12 half steps in an octave, and any introduction of a whole step will result in replacing two half steps. We will stipulate that our system excludes scales with two adjacent half steps, as well as intervals larger than a whole step. (We can always add chromatic passing tones, as in "bebop" scales, or leave out tones, as in pentatonic scales.)

The *whole tone scale* fills the octave with 6 notes, arranged in 6 whole steps and zero half steps. 7-note scales with 5 whole steps and 2 half steps form the majority of scales in our system. The *diminished scale* uses 8 notes, arranged with 4 whole steps and 4 half steps. Scales with 6, 8, 10, or 12 half steps are excluded from our system because they would have to contain adjacent half steps.

Now consider the 7-note scales, which make up the bulk of our chord scale system. We can demonstrate that *the 14 modes of major and melodic minor* include all of the possible orderings of 5 whole steps and 2 half steps that we can use to fill an octave. The easiest way to show this is by the process of elimination.

Below, these 14 scales are listed according to their structure—first the group beginning half/whole/half, then half/whole/whole, and so forth. It can be seen that every possible ordering is included, and that each scale has a name in our system.

altered (or superlocrian, or diminished whole tone)

locrian

phrygian

dorian ♭2

locrian ♯2

aeolian (natural minor)

dorian

melodic minor

mixolydian ♭6

mixolydian

ionian (major)

lydian dominant

lydian

lydian augmented

For another perspective, consider the diagrams below. The first circle represents the interval spacing of a major scale (in this case C) and its modes. Major (ionian) begins at C ("12 o'clock") and goes clockwise; dorian begins at the spot marked D, etc. The second circle represents the interval spacing of melodic minor, and its modes.

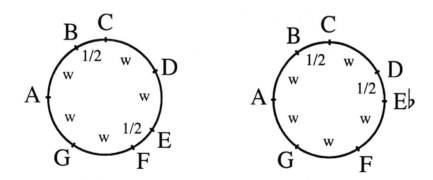

There are no other ways to arrange a circle with two half steps and five steps, no half steps adjacent. Thus, these patterns generate all possible '

In mathematical terms, there is no reason to think of "major" and "melodic minor" as starting points for generating the system. We could just as easily have started with locrian instead of major, and lydian augmented instead of melodic minor, as the sources for generating the other modes. The only reason that we think of major and melodic minor as basic is that most musicians are already familiar with them.

The use of melodic minor modes in jazz was pioneered in the 1950s by George Russell, who thought of them as generated by lydian augmented. Some current theory books still present this viewpoint. And as for the modes of major: Dorian, phrygian, lydian, and mixolydian (the "church modes") were recognized as scales centuries before major or minor!

A note for the mathematically inclined: The question of determining how many ways you can arrange 2 half steps and 5 whole steps in an octave (no adjacent half steps) is exactly the same as the question, "How many different ways can we arrange 5 blue beads and 2 red beads in a necklace, no red beads touching?" The circular diagrams, above, should make this obvious. The formula to solve this kind of "circular permutation" problem is

$$P = \frac{n!}{a!b!} - c$$

where P is the number of permutations (in this case, different scale patterns), n is the number of elements (steps in the scale), a is one type of element (half steps), b is another type (whole steps), and c is the number of possibilities to be excluded (possible positions of adjacent half steps).

In our musical problem, this works out as

$$\frac{7!}{2!5!} - 7$$

or, $21 - 7 = 14$ (different 7-note scales)

My thanks to Randy Smith for the concept of this appendix and the circle diagrams, and to Delphine LeCocq for the formula.

Appendix C

Solos for Bb and Eb instruments; chord charts for play-along tracks

In this section are:

- Bb and Eb transpositions of the three sample solos, and

- chord charts for concert, Bb, and Eb instruments for each of the three play-along tracks (blues, Rhythm changes, and "After You've Gone").

Depending on your instrument, you may sometimes need to shift notes up or down an octave in the sample solos.

Note: The blues solos are printed without a key signature; all accidentals are notated in the melodic line. All the chord charts are shown this way, too.

Bb instruments: Blues in G (F concert)

E♭ instruments: Blues in D (F concert)

B♭ instruments: Rhythm changes in C (B♭ concert)

E♭ instruments: Rhythm changes in G (B♭ concert)

B♭ instruments: "After You've Gone" in D (C concert)

(begin next solo)

E♭ instruments: "After You've Gone" in A (C concert)

(begin next solo)

C instruments: Blues in F

B♭ instruments: Blues in G (F concert)

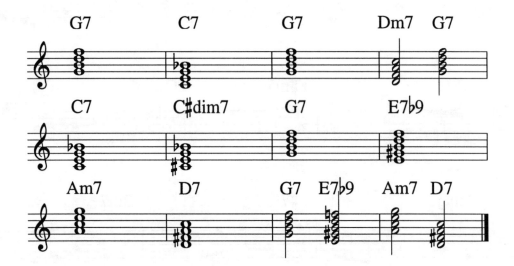

E♭ instruments: Blues in D (F concert)

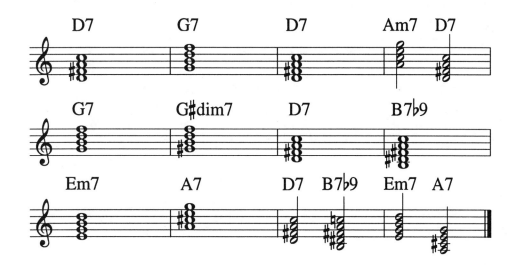

C instruments: Rhythm changes in B♭

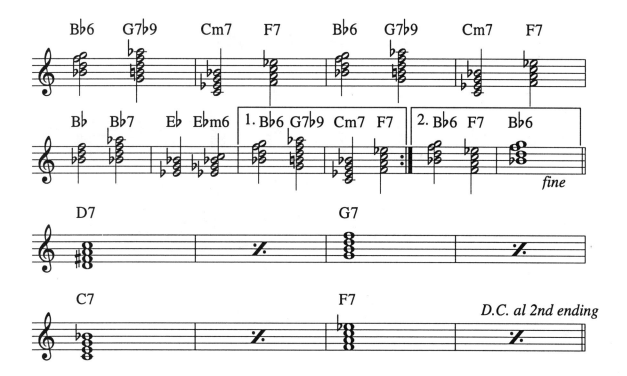

B♭ instruments: Rhythm changes in C (B♭ concert)

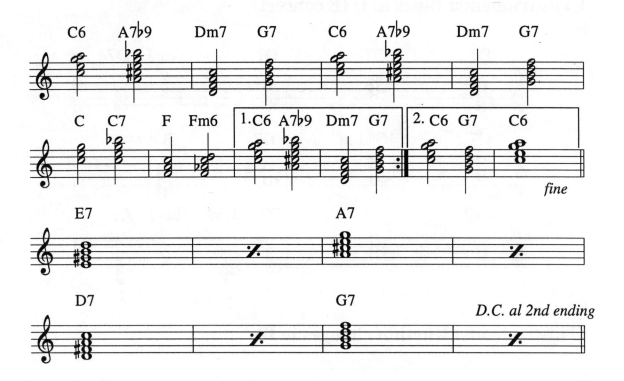

E♭ instruments: Rhythm changes in G (B♭ concert)

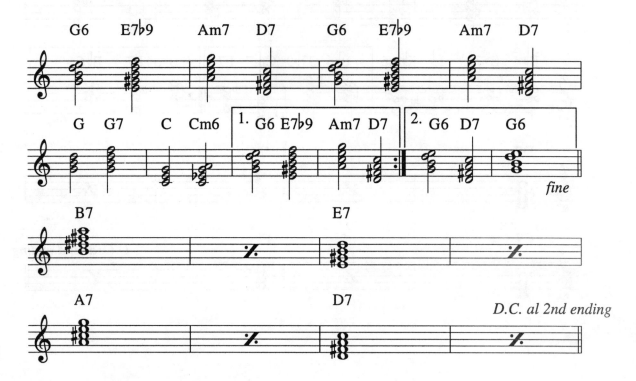

C instruments: "After You've Gone" in C

B♭ instruments: "After You've Gone" in D (C concert)

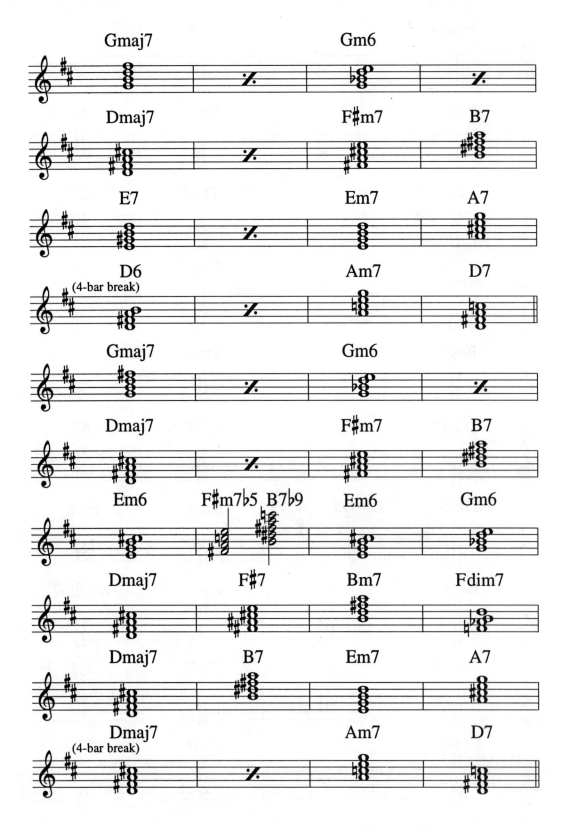

E♭ instruments: "After You've Gone" in A (C concert)

Appendix D

Selected bibliography

Below is a short list of books that you might find especially useful. Also valuable: classical theory texts, jazz history books, historical and instructional videos, and educational software. The very best source for information is, of course, the music itself, in the jazz section of your local CD store and library.

Theory:

David Baker. *Jazz Improvisation*. Baker is one of the most prolific writers in jazz education; this book is a good example of his work. See Baker's many other books, also.

Andrew Jaffe. *Jazz Harmony*.

Mark Levine. *The Jazz Piano Book*.

Mark Levine. *The Jazz Theory Book*.

Scott Reeves. *Creative Jazz Improvisation*.

Walt Weiskopf and Ramon Ricker. *Coltrane: A Player's Guide to His Harmony*. A nice explanation of "Coltrane changes," a topic that I decided was just past the scope of this book.

Patterns:

Jerry Coker, Gary Campbell, Jimmy Casale, and Jerry Greene. *Patterns for Jazz*. The definitive patterns book. Coker has written several other excellent jazz instruction books.

Oliver Nelson. *Patterns for Improvisation*. This was one of the first patterns books. Read the introduction.

Transcriptions:

Jamey Aebersold and Ken Slone. *Charlie Parker Omnibook*. Solos from one of jazz's greatest improvisers. Parker's musical vocabulary is a basic part of the jazz language.

Fake books:

Chuck Sher. *The New Real Book*, Vols. 1, 2, and 3. Some of the best jazz-oriented fake books currently available (volume 1 is the most useful). The original, bootleg *Real Book*, first printed in the early 1970's, is still a standard reference in the jazz world—however, it is full of errors, and was printed with no regard for copyrights. Sher's books are more carefully produced, as well as being legal.

Sue Mingus, ed./Jazz Workshop. *Charles Mingus: More Than a Fake Book*. Definitive versions of 55 Mingus compositions, with performance and biographical notes. All fake books should be this good.

Play-alongs:

Jamey Aebersold. *A New Approach to Jazz Improvisation*. The famous series of jazz play-along CDs, now about 90 volumes. Each volume centers on a different musical subject, or composer.

Dix Bruce/Mel Bay Publications. *Backup Trax*.

Bill Dobbins/Advance Music. *The Jazz Workshop Series*.

PG Music. *Band in a Box*. Software for creating play-alongs on computer.

General reading:

Paul Berliner. *Thinking in Jazz: The Infinite Art of Improvisation*. A comprehensive study of the way jazz greats learned to improvise, and the thought processes behind the music.

Scott DeVeaux. *The Birth of Bebop*. Examines a crucial period in jazz history, the years that led to the development of bop, with particular attention to Coleman Hawkins' career and style. Great historical writing and analysis.